Praise for *Human Resource Management: Optimizing Organizational Performance*

"This well-written compendium is a must on the shelves of all educational leaders who work with human resource management. Easy to read, this book is chock-full of insights that will be beneficial for all administrators."

—**Charles Russo**, CJR, JD, EdD,
Joseph Panzer Chair in Education;
research professor of law; director, PhD program in
educational leadership, University of Dayton, Ohio

"The role of human resources is critical to all school districts and companies and this book is a practical and understandable resource. The authors present an excellent step-by-step process for establishing and managing those elements essential to effective HR management. I highly recommend this book."

—**Fred G. Parrish**, president and CEO,
The Profit Experts

"The authors provide an excellent basis for understanding human resource management. I'm confident that this book will provide a positive contribution to education."

—**Susan Sosoo**, EdD, AP, administration/organization,
New York City Department of Education, New York

"The authors provide an excellent basis for understanding human resource management. I am confident that this book will provide a positive contribution to the field of education."

—**Dr. Bill Robertson**, superintendent of schools,
Fremont School District 79

"Tomal and Schilling have done a brilliant job of writing a smart, practical book. This is essential reading for educators who want to advance their knowledge of human resource management."

—**Dr. Claudia Santin**, dean and professor of leadership,
College of Business, Concordia University Chicago

"As a principal with a strong interest in human resource management, I found this book to be extremely practical, well thought-out, and an excellent overall guide for anyone looking to go into this field."

—**Jeff Knapp**, principal, Rockland School,
Libertyville School District 70, Illinois

"A new, fresh, and engaging approach to human resource management with an emphasis on true management skills and a long overdue guide that sets a new standard for the public and private sector. This book is not only to a great consult to actually use, but is enriching, engaging, and a relevant presentation of the key elements of successful human resource management. Tomal and Schilling have captured the essence of resource management for today. They set a new standard for others to follow—you won't be disappointed."

—**Michael Harkins**, professor of history,
William Rainey Harper College, Palatine, Illinois;
president of the Illinois conference of the AAUP

"The educational environment is consistently involved in a variety of change processes, often with limited financial resources. This is an outstanding guidebook filled with practical strategies and solutions for managing human capital and improving school district operations—a must-read for all teachers and administrators."

—**George Zimmer**, EdD, associate professor,
Concordia University Chicago

"The authors provide an excellent basis for understanding and applying human resource management. I highly recommend this book to all educators and companies who want to advance their knowledge and mastery. Most outstanding!"

—**Robert N. L. Browning**, founder and CEO,
Success Solutions International

"This is a thoughtful and comprehensive volume refining our understanding of school human resources for student achievement and success. The practical strategies offered make this a fascinating book that will provide new insights into school administration. It is an invaluable resource for educators no matter their level of experience."

—**Dr. Robert Libka**,
school central office administrator, retired

"I congratulate Drs. Tomal and Schilling on this sterling accomplishment. This is a good read for those serious about school improvement and increasing the effectiveness and efficiency of any school or schools."

—**R. E. Everett**, PhD, executive director, retired,
Illinois Association of School Business Officials

"The authors have provided an outstanding book on understanding human resources with clear, concise, and concrete examples that anyone can relate to."

—**Dr. Curtis A. Smith**, professor;
former assistant to the deputy superintendent,
Chicago Public Schools

"Human resources play a pivotal role in the success of school improvement in detecting and securing the best qualified teacher and leadership candidates. I highly recommend this book to all educators who want to advance their knowledge in human resource management. This book is outstanding!"

—**Dr. Beverly A. Hives**, school leadership intervention
specialist/AU/MD K–2/Cleveland Metropolitan
School District, Ohio

"Dr. Tomal and Dr. Schilling have done it again. This is an excellent resource for students of school human resources. It unpacks a myriad of topics and brings clarity to a complex topic. A must-read for all aspiring and existing school leaders."

—**Jeffrey T. Brierton**, PhD, author, professor, and
school consultant; former teacher, administrator, and
high school principal

"This book provides both theoretically sound and practically valuable insights into human resource management. It is an outstanding and instructive tool for school and business leaders."

—**Dr. Brenda F. Graham**, former school district
superintendent; professor, Department of Leadership,
Concordia University Chicago

"An exemplary book on managing human resources in the school organization. The critical piece to a successful school district is how are people managed, supported, and treated, legally and professionally. This well-presented book addresses these issues and more. Required reading for anyone providing leadership to an organization."

—**Dr. A. Donald Hendricks**,
former school superintendent, Illinois

"Human resource management employs an ideal theory-to-practice approach to provide current and aspiring administrators with the necessary tools for effective leadership. This comprehensive yet succinct content makes this essential reading for all school human resource managers and school leaders."

—**Dr. Sandra Coyner**, professor of education;
past ATEA editor, The University of Akron

"An excellent book on human resource management and collective bargaining for all school administrators and graduate students in school leadership."

—**Dr. Robert Wilhite**, dean, College of
Graduate Studies, Concordia University Chicago

"There is no more important job responsibility for school leaders than the proper management of human resources. This book provides a framework for understanding the basics of selection, development, compensation, and management. I recommend it as a tool for training administrators and as a handy resource for HR professionals."

—**Dr. Robert F. Schultz**, human resource
trainer and consultant, Westerville, Ohio

Human Resource Management

The Concordia University Chicago Leadership Series

An Educational Series from Rowman Littlefield Education

Series Editor: Daniel R. Tomal, PhD

Education leaders have many titles and positions in American schools today: professors, K–12 teachers, district and building administrators, teacher coaches, teacher evaluators, directors, coordinators, staff specialists, and so on. More than ever, educators need practical and proven educational and leadership resources to stay current and advance the learning of students.

The Concordia University Chicago Leadership Series is a unique resource that addresses this need. The authors of this series are award-winning authors and scholars who are both passionate theorists and practitioners of this valuable collection of works. They give realistic and real-life examples and strategies to help all educators inspire and make a difference in school improvement and student learning that get results.

This Leadership Series consists of a variety of distinctive books on subjects of school change, research, completing advanced degrees, school administration, leadership and motivation, business finance and resources, human resource management, challenging students to learn, action research for practitioners, the teacher as a coach, school law and policies, ethics, and many other topics that are critical to modern educators in meeting the emerging and diverse students of today. These books also align with current federal, state, and various association accreditation standards and elements.

Staying current and building the future require the knowledge and strategies presented in these books. The Leadership Series originator Daniel R. Tomal, PhD, an award-winning author who has published over 20 books and 200 articles and studies, is a highly sought-after speaker and educational researcher. He, along with his coauthors, provide a wealth of educational experience, proven strategies that can help all educators aspire to be the best they can be in meeting the demands of modern educational leadership.

Human Resource Management

Optimizing Organizational Performance

Second Edition

Daniel R. Tomal and Craig A. Schilling

ROWMAN & LITTLEFIELD
Lanham • Boulder • New York • London

Published by Rowman & Littlefield
An imprint of The Rowman & Littlefield Publishing Group, Inc.
4501 Forbes Boulevard, Suite 200, Lanham, Maryland 20706
www.rowman.com

6 Tinworth Street, London SE11 5AL, United Kingdom

British Library Cataloguing in Publication Information Available

Library of Congress Cataloging-in-Publication Data Available

ISBN: 978-1-4758-4404-7 (cloth : alk. paper)
ISBN: 978-1-4758-4405-4 (pbk. : alk. paper)
ISBN: 978-1-4758-4406-1 (electronic)

♾™ The paper used in this publication meets the minimum requirements of American National Standard for Information Sciences—Permanence of Paper for Printed Library Materials, ANSI/NISO Z39.48–1992.

Printed in the United States of America

Other Books by Daniel R. Tomal and Craig A. Schilling

Resource Management for School Administrators: Optimizing Fiscal, Facility, and Human Resources (2013)

Managing Human Resources and Collective Bargaining (2013)

Leading School Change: Maximizing Resources for School Improvement (2013)

The Teacher Leader: Core Competencies and Strategies for Effective Leadership (2014)

Leading with Resolve and Mastery: Competency-Based Strategies for Superintendent Success (2017)

Forthcoming

Managing and Optimizing School Resources, 2nd Edition (2019)

Contents

Foreword

For many, many years the role of school business manager, regardless of its plethora of other titles, has been perceived as one primarily dealing with accounting and finance. This can be demonstrated by reviewing the job descriptions and the available published literature of the 1960s and 1970s. Unfortunately, the profession of school business management contributed to this misperception.

Over the past thirty years the growth in the number of tasks and functions assigned and performed by the school business manager has been significant. Not only this growth in responsibilities but also the growing understanding of the relationship between the use of resources and student achievement has brought the position of school business manager into the spotlight.

The need and opportunities for the incumbent and the new career seeker in school business management for professional development has not always kept pace with that of "what and how" the school business manager is expected to perform at a high level. This is true at the university level and at the association level and in the United States and abroad. Degree programs specific to school business management and state certification requirements have been narrow and/or nonexistent. In the past, there were few universities that did offer graduate degrees in school business management.

The major degree was basically a master's degree in Educational Administration (the usual principalship course offering), an additional finance and accounting course, and in some instances a facility course. In this day and age this is clearly inadequate for what society needs as far as trained school business managers go.

Scholarly field-based research in the total domain of school business management which could serve as the basis for a knowledge base reflected through a body of literature has been lacking. Over the past several decades, publications that treat in a comprehensive fashion all elements of school business management have started to appear. This work by Professors Daniel R. Tomal and Craig A. Schilling is a welcome addition to the literature relating to school business management. What make this text such a valuable addition to our literature?

First, both Dr. Tomal and Dr. Schilling are scholar-practitioners. Both have followed career paths that many would find hard to duplicate. Both have served in the profession with distinction, worked in the trenches, and thereby gained an experience base that is clearly reflected in their work. Both have served their profession in leadership positions at the local, state, national, and international levels and made significant contributions at each level.

Second, the overall organization of each chapter has been thoughtfully laid out. All chapters have been written in a consistent format, and the sequence of content has been consistent in scope and relevancy.

Third, the book has been written in a practical approach, offering strategies that are straightforward and easy to apply. All the numerous principles and strategies have been developed from a research/theoretical base and then accompanied with a comprehensive summary of chapter topics, case studies, exercises, and discussion questions that are well thought out, clearly defined, and thought-provoking. The material is not "busy-work" for the students who are serious about their study of school business management or for incumbent school business managers seeking to improve their own performance and enhance their value to their employer.

Fourth, the reference section that follows each chapter provides a rich starting point for the reader who wants to take a deeper journey into the chapter topic. The references also demonstrate that the authors are current and familiar with the field.

Fifth, each chapter begins with a set of objectives that are cross-referenced to the standards of PSEL (Professional Standards for Educational Leadership) and ELCC (Educational Leadership Constituent Council). The content of each chapter then supports the objectives in a clear and succinct manner.

Sixth, it is a book that can serve well those who work at all levels of education such as universities and public, private, and charter school systems. While reference and appendices reflect heavily on the standards, laws, and practices in the United States, this book has utility beyond the U.S. borders and in fact it can be a source of reflection and impact on any school in positive ways. What may not be required in one setting may still have use as a voluntary paradigm in another.

I congratulate Drs. Tomal and Schilling on this sterling accomplishment. This is a good read for those serious about school improvement and increasing the effectiveness and efficiency of any school or organization. It is a welcome addition to our literature. It will serve as a great tool for those who are shaping the minds of the next generation of school business managers.

R. E. Everett, PhD
Professor of School Business Management—Retired,
Northern Illinois University;
Executive Director—Retired,
Illinois Association of School Business Officials
DeKalb, Illinois

Preface

Human resource management is one of the most critical responsibilities of all organizational leaders. This book has been written based upon years of study, research, and consulting, in school administration and companies. The strategies described in this book have been found successful in operating at the school district, school building level, and companies and is especially centered on providing information on the connecting human resource management and organizational performance.

While primarily directed toward public schools, the strategies in this book can also be effective for private elementary and secondary schools, charter schools, and any organization. The information and strategies are practical and useful techniques that can be used by any school administrator or graduate of human resources and collective bargaining student, who desire to optimize human resources.

Chapter 1 provides practical strategies for human resource planning. Extensive examples are provided in developing strategic plans, succession planning, and how to plan successors for incumbent positions. Lastly, a comprehensive description of Federal Equal Employment Opportunity Commission laws and executive orders are given with practical examples on how they impact human resource management.

Chapter 2 covers the recruiting and selecting applicants. Topics include methods of recruiting, selecting the best candidates, and laws and policies. Several examples and sample forms are also included in this chapter.

Chapter 3 includes the topic of the mentoring of new employees. Also, professional development, learning and growth frameworks, establishing and conducting performance appraisal system, and alternative evaluation programs are included. Practical examples and forms are provided in this chapter. A challenging and realistic case study is included at the end of the chapter to test the comprehension of the material.

Chapter 4 covers the topic of leading and motivating employees. Relevant topics, such as principles of leadership, are covered. Several popular leadership theories such as situational leadership, the X and Y model, the Leadership Grid, Expectancy Model, Two-factor Motivational Theory, the Equity Motivation Model, Team Leadership, and Total Quality Management are presented as they relate to school leadership.

The topics of building collaboration and disciplining employees are covered in chapter 5. Other topics include managing conflict and terminating employees. Several practical examples and forms are also provided, and the chapter concludes with a comprehensive case study.

Chapter 6 includes the topics of benefits and compensation. Several areas including establishing benefits and compensation programs, salary structures, and types of compensation programs are discussed. Several exhibits and examples of compensation programs are provided.

Chapter 7 covers the topic of unions and collective bargaining. This chapter also includes the history of unions, negotiation strategies, and the collective bargaining process. There are also case situations and practical examples of collective bargaining in the chapter. There is a challenging, concluding case study that can be helpful in understanding and applying the principles and strategies in the chapter.

Chapter 8 includes the area of managing human resources, core competencies of human resources professionals, conducting audits, creating efficiencies, position control, and technology. Several process mapping and technology checklists are included. Several illustrations and a comprehensive case study are included at the end of the chapter.

At the end of the book there are several helpful resources. Some of these include employee rights, employer and union rights and obligations, a summary of major laws, laws enforced by the United States Equal Employment Opportunity Commission (EEOC), prohibited employment policies, and practices of the EEOC. These reference materials can be very useful in understanding governmental policies, laws, and executive orders regulating human resources.

FEATURES OF THE BOOK

Nothing can be worse than reading a book that is boring, dry, and impractical for educators. This book is unique in that it provides many engaging examples that can be used by all educators. One feature of the book is the correlation of the objectives of each chapter with professional organizational standards of the *Educational Leadership Constituent Council* (ELCC) and the Professional Standards for Educational Leaders (PSEL).

Another valuable feature of the book is the incorporation of many diverse strategies related to school leadership; motivation, recruiting, and selecting candidates; and disciplining, compensating and bargaining, and terminating employees. They are provided in a straightforward and practical manner. The topics in this book are useful for any administrator who desires to optimize fiscal, facility, and human resources.

Other features of this book include:

- Practical examples of human resource management
- Examples of basic school compensation structures
- Strategies for leading and motivating employees in the school environment
- Models of leadership and motivational theories that have been proven in the business world as applied to the educational setting
- A comprehensive description of conducting strategic and succession planning of up-to-date guidelines, EEOC laws, and legal considerations
- Practical strategies in giving employees feedback and taking action for improvement
- Examples of discipline offenses and how to administer disciplinary action
- A review of some of the major federal and state laws and guidelines
- Strategies in managing conflict and how to promote teamwork and collaboration
- Strategies in collective bargaining

Lastly, this book also contains a rich source of educational and reference materials so that educators can apply the concepts for school resource management. Some materials include:

- Case illustrations and figures in applying leadership and human resource strategies
- Examples of motivation strategies that can improve academic performance
- A sample of field-based educational issues
- Actual examples of assessments and real-life case studies

ORGANIZATION OF THE BOOK

The organization of this book has been written in a straightforward manner so educators can understand the critical school resource management. Each chapter builds upon the other. However, each chapter is also distinct in itself because it covers a specific topic that relates to the three topics. Lastly, each chapter includes basic theories and examples of applying these theories, and case studies and exercises and discussion.

Acknowledgments

Appreciation is extended to the many people who have assisted and worked with the authors. Special appreciation is given to the authors' students, colleagues, and former business associates in the corporate world. Lastly, the authors would like to extend gratitude to the many people who endorsed this book and provided insight for this project.

Chapter 1

Human Resource Planning

Objectives

At the conclusion of this chapter you will be able to:

1. Understand the human resource planning process (ELCC 3.3, PSEL 1, 3).
2. Define the steps of strategic and succession planning (ELCC 3.3, PSEL 1, 3).
3. Understand critical team values necessary to collaboratively develop a vision and effectively manage human resources (ELCC 1.1, 1.2, 1.3, 5.1, 5.2, 5. 3, PSEL 1, 2, 3, 5).
4. Define critical laws and executive orders of the Equal Employment Opportunity Commission (EEOC; ELCC 6.1, 6.2, 6.3, PSEL 3, 6).
5. Describe how EEOC laws and regulations impact human resource planning (ELCC 6.1, 6.2, 6.3, PSEL 3, 6).

STRATEGIC PLANNING

Human resource management consists of a multiplicity of responsibilities that are vital to all organizations. Key to the human resource function is ensuring that there are adequate and qualified people in the best positions to achieve a thriving and successful organization. One way to help meet this objective is through effective human resource planning. There are three key planning functions that are presented in this chapter, which are strategic planning, forecasting, and succession planning (see figure 1.1).

Strategic planning is a common activity of most organizations and can help to ensure that all resources are identified as required by the organization. While there are many facets to managing human resources, the foundation

Figure 1.1. Three key planning areas of human resources.

begins with good strategic planning. There is an old adage which states, "Those who fail to plan, plan to fail." Planning in human resources involves assessing organizational needs, predicting the future, establishing and communicating operational goals, conducting job analyses, and identifying key positions needed by the organization.

Human resource planning ensures that an organization has the correct number of people in the right places at the right time who have the necessary skills and performance to complete the institution's objectives. An organization cannot accomplish any goals without qualified people. In education, it also means human resource planning is aligning staffing needs with the needs of students to increase performance.

Proper planning allows administrators to ensure successful transitions and ensure that people can accomplish the tasks needed of an organization in a smooth and harmonious manner. While some school districts approach human resource planning differently, all administrators need to be involved in human resource forecasting to ensure that there are capable people performing the necessary tasks of the organization.

Strategic planning is one of the most popular strategies utilized by educators to prepare a comprehensive plan for meeting workforce needs for the future (see figure 1.2). Essentially, strategic planning involves answering the questions of "What is our situation today?" "Where do we want to go?" "How

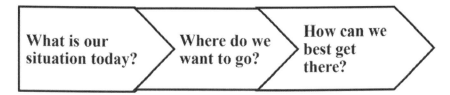

Figure 1.2. Three fundamental questions for strategic planning.

can we best get there?" and "Who are the people who are going to champion the strategies in getting us there?"

Strategic planning is a technique that originated in corporate America and has become a popular tool in education. This process allows administrators to identify critical issues that need addressed, establish an overall vision, develop critical goals and key strategies to accomplish the vision, establish metrics to measure performance, and plan resources.

Some of the benefits of strategic planning include:

1. Builds upon collaboration and the expertise of people.
2. Allows for creativity in addressing major issues.
3. Stimulates visionary thinking to improve an organization.
4. Provides empowerment for people to accomplish goals.
5. Improves the performance of the organization and helps in predicting financial budgets for a school district.

While strategic planning has many benefits, it needs to be undertaken in a structured manner. If managed poorly, the costs of strategic planning can exceed the benefits. Individuals may waste valuable time in brainstorming ideas that are unproductive if the process is not facilitated well. Some limitations include: people may concentrate on the most immediate needs without regard for long-term needs, administrators may fail in successfully implementing strategies, poor accountability, lack of resources, and lack of follow-up to the strategic initiatives.

Therefore, when strategic planning is undertaken, proper resources are needed to ensure success. Some of these resources include providing sufficient time to develop the strategic plan, allowing for creativity, selecting proper people who will participate and develop the plan, and providing sufficient financial resources to implement the strategic plan. Good preparations for the strategic planning activity and proper allocation of resources are keys to the success of the overall effort.

The procedure for conducting strategic planning can vary from organization to organization. Typically, strategic planning should begin at the top level and then be facilitated throughout the entire organization. For example, strategic planning may start at the district level, conducted at the school building level, and then conducted at the department level. In this way all organizational units are supporting the top district-level initiatives. However, strategic planning can be independently conducted at the school building level as long as the people understand the established goals of the district.

The process of conducting *strategic planning* involves several critical steps:

1. *Assemble the team.* Select the members of the strategic planning team.
2. *Determine resources and logistics.* Agree on the logistics and resources needed for completing the strategic plan.
3. *Determine format.* Agree on the final format and components of the strategic plan.
4. *Write values statement.* Discuss critical values and behaviors and formulate a values statement for the organization.
5. *Write a vision statement.* Write a vision statement, and if necessary, a mission statement.
6. *Complete a SWOT analysis.* Complete a detailed SWOT analysis.
7. *Write major goals.* Write major goals for the strategic plan based upon the SWOT items.
8. *Prioritize major goals.* Prioritize the major goals and determine timeframes (1, 3, 5 years).
9. *Write key strategies.* Develop key strategies for each of the major goals.
10. *Include metrics.* Include metrics (measurable score cards or performance indicators) for each strategic goal and financial estimates for funding key strategies.
11. *Assign champions.* Assign champions to major goals to be accountable for them.
12. *Write the strategic plan.* Write the strategic plan and gain approval.
13. *Integrate the strategic plan into the performance management system.* The goals and people who are accountable should be included into the goal-setting and appraisal process.
14. *Conduct awareness sessions.* Inform people of the strategic plan their roles. Get people involved into the process and implement the strategic plan.
15. *Monitor and assess progress.* Establish a system of monitoring the progress of the strategic plan and documenting results.
16. *Conduct reviews of individuals' performance.* Conduct individual mid-year and year-end reviews of people and the goals. Provide rewards and incentives.
17. *Evaluate the strategic planning process.* Evaluate what went well and not so well with the strategic planning process and improve the process for next time.

The first step is to assemble the strategic planning team. Typically, this team will consist of the top administrator (e.g., superintendent or principal) and his or her administrators and selected teachers and staff members. This team will not only be responsible for developing the final product but will also be critical in driving the process and determining the resources that are needed for completing the strategic plan, step two.

Typically this team will meet to plan all the resources needed and decide whether an outside facilitator will be used for the process. The use of an outside facilitator can be helpful in allowing the entire team to concentrate on the content of the plan rather than needing to facilitate and record all the information which can be done by the facilitator.

The facilitator can also conduct the process, reduce pressure from superiors, and help keep the group on track. While there may be costs in utilizing an outside facilitator, this person can be valuable in providing input regarding his or her experience in conducting strategic planning with other organizations as well as helping the team when they encounter difficult interpersonal and process issues.

The strategic plan is a road map for the organization and should include specific human resource initiatives that support the educational goals of the district. The strategic plan should also be a comprehensive document which supports all the units of the entire organization such as building facilities, human resources, equipment and supplies, engineering, technology, financial and budgeting resources, and educational programs and materials.

The School Improvement Plan (SIP) is similar to strategic planning, but it generally centers on student learning such as curriculum and instruction, student and faculty programs, and student behavior that impacts the school. Therefore the strategic plan is the overall road map that includes all these facets in operating a school district or school.

The third step necessitates the team agreeing upon an acceptable format for the *strategic plan document*. There are many variations in the components comprised in a strategic plan. For example, some schools may not have both a vision and mission statement. Also depending upon the complexity of a school district, the number of departmental or unit plans can vary. There may also be a plan for all the essential units of an organization such as academic departments, engineering department, transportation, safety and security, custodial, and so forth. The components of a strategic plan might consist of the following:

1. Executive summary
2. Table of contents
3. Core competencies
4. SWOT analysis

5. Critical success factors
6. Vision statement (and mission statement)
7. Major goals
8. Key strategies and financial needs
9. Metrics (performance indicators)
10. Department-level goals and strategies
11. Status summary spreadsheet
12. Appendix

It is important that the team determine the logistics in completing the strategic plan such as how often they will meet, location, schedule, and materials and resources. Some teams may schedule multiple sessions, which range from two to four hours over an extended period of time such as six weeks. However, other teams may conduct a retreat where they may spend a couple concentrated days developing the plan. Each team must decide the overall logistics that are best for them and least obtrusive to the operation of the school.

Step four involves the team constructing a *values statement*. It is important to establish the key values that drive the behavior of people within the organization. Establishing values is a prerequisite to writing a *vision statement*. For example, if the school is a religious-based organization, the values will be different than a public institution.

Establishing these values can help in crafting the ultimate vision and mission statements. When examining the values, some of the questions that can help guide the team include "What values are important to us?" "What do we stand for?" "What specific behaviors do we value?" "How do we desire to treat each other?" and "How do we want to be viewed by our stakeholders?" Typically, by answering these questions, a team will arrive at a values statement. In addition, team members can participate in *values exercises* to establish common team values for the group.

Described next is a list of typical values that team members could review and rank in order of importance for their team's success in working together in a group.

- Achievement (achieving and exceeding our school or organizational goals)
- Altruism (giving of our time, passion, energy, and commitment)
- Collaboration (teamwork and working well with others)
- Creativity (being innovative, offering new ideas, change)
- Honesty and trust (being honest and trustworthy with each other)
- Justice (fairness and respect to each other)
- Knowledge (continued learning beyond what we already know)

- Commitment (total faithfulness to each other and school or company)
- Morality (doing the right thing, having good ethics)
- Power (ability to get what you want)

For example, in this exercise the team members might determine that a value of *individual power* can be destructive to the overall cohesiveness of the team. In other words, the team members may decide that seeking individual power should be restrained, while other values such as *honesty* and *trust* should be encouraged and reinforced for achieving team success for the organization.

Step five, writing the *vision statement*, typically includes thoughtful reflection regarding the desired culture of the organization. Some helpful statements consist of "Striving for the highest quality learning within the school," "Striving to treat each other fairly through honesty, respect and open communications," "Providing an opportunity for everyone to grow professionally," or "Having a passion for innovation, originality, and continued intellectual growth."

Some teams may elect to write a *mission* statement in addition to a vision statement. Either a *vision statement* or a *mission statement*, or both, can be written. A mission statement tends to be a broad goal such as "To explore the galaxies." Many organizations have a mission statement and use it to give general descriptive information regarding their purpose and as a statement of expression.

A vision statement is typically much more concrete such as "To land a person on the moon and watch him or her walk." While the statements are similar, the vision statement concentrates more on behaviors and is often more concrete and measurable. For example, a school district may have a mission statement such as "To allow all students to grow to their fullest capacity," versus a vision statement such as "All students will score in the top 20 percent of the nation on standardized tests." However all organizations are unique organisms and need to determine what kind of vision and mission statements best reflects the desires of the stakeholders.

Step six consists of completing the SWOT analysis. SWOT stands for *strengths, weaknesses, opportunities,* and *threats.* In this step, the team identifies the *strengths* of the school. Examples include a good core reputation, strong leadership, competent and experienced teachers, and high employee morale and satisfaction.

Weaknesses might include lack of technology equipment and competencies, inadequate facilities, poor safety, and inadequate transportation for students. *Opportunities* are those situations that offer potential additional support to the school district in achieving higher performance levels that include establishing business relationships, utilizing university expertise, writing grants, and increasing financial resources.

Threats are typically situations that might hinder the success of the school district that could include an aging faculty, high employee attrition, political unrest within the community, and potential high immigrant growth that may require additional programs and resources. Establishing the *strengths*, *weaknesses*, *opportunities*, and *threats* can become the basis from which the strategic plan is developed.

Often, the *strengths* are recognized and sometimes improved, but the *weaknesses* need to be addressed by establishing concrete *goals* and *key strategies*. In addition, *opportunities* and *threats* need to be examined, and strategic goals can be written based upon them. The opportunities often emerge from the examination of the weaknesses. Also, the threats should be identified as internal and external threats in achieving goals and opportunities.

Step seven entails writing the *major goals* for the strategic plan. These major goals should be written using SMART criteria. SMART goals consist of being *specific*, *measurable*, *attainable*, *realistic*, and *timely*. Once the major goals are written, it is important to carefully examine the goals and prioritize them, step eight. A team may write too many goals that cannot be realistically achieved. The team members should decide which are the highest priority goals and establish time frames for each of the goals such as one-, three-, or five-year increments.

Step eight, prioritizing the major goals and establishing time frames for goals, involves negotiation, collaboration, and resource management. Team members need to be respectful of each other and establish *ground rules* in how they conduct themselves in the meetings. Typical functional behaviors include seeking and giving opinions, elaborating and encouraging people to praise others, and being open to new ideas. Nonfunctional behaviors are being too aggressive, self-confessing, playing politics, pushing self-interest above the group, withdrawal, or clowning around and disrupting the group.

Once the major goals are written, *key strategies* must be developed, step nine. "A goal cannot be done." For example, if someone wants to become a millionaire, the *key strategy* outlines the process in "how to get the money?" If a major school goal is to advance the knowledge and technical skills of the faculty, then one *key strategy* might be to hire a technology consultant and to conduct technology training sessions.

Also, included within the strategy should be well-written *metrics*, step ten. *Metrics*, sometimes called *performance indicators*, are the scorecards upon which the level of performance is to be established. For example, if the major goal is to improve technological knowledge and the key strategy is to provide training for people, a metric might be to achieve 50 percent competency within three months.

Step eleven requires assigning *champions* to the goals so that people can be held accountable for accomplishing them. *Champions* act as crusaders in promoting the goals, providing resources needed to accomplish the goals, and measuring the results. Without passionate champions supporting the goals, it is easy to lack the follow-through necessary to achieve them.

The champions for the goals may or may not include members of the strategic planning team, and they should periodically meet to review their progress. Champions should be selected based upon the criteria of high credibility and strong desire for achieving results. They also should be people who have good interpersonal skills and who can work collaboratively with people to support their efforts in accomplishing the goals.

Step twelve involves *writing the strategic plan*, which requires careful review and editing by the members of the team to produce the final document. Outside readers can be obtained to help critique the final document and ensure that it is of acceptable quality and standards and that it is in line with federal and state policies and guidelines. The final strategic plan is often approved by the strategic planning team, superintendent, or school board.

Step thirteen consists of integrating a strategic plan into the *performance management system.* This entails selecting the key goals and people and to hold them accountable through the goal setting and performance appraisal process. This step is often overlooked in the strategic planning process. It is important that there is linkage between the goals and individuals' goals, so people can be evaluated based upon the results. In some organizations actual bonuses are established and given to individuals who exceed the goals, which provide incentives for meeting and exceeding the goals.

Step fourteen involves making everyone aware of the strategic plan. The plan is not going to be accepted or worthwhile if it is locked up in a cabinet and no one knows about it. The strategic plan is a living document that should be integrated within the entire organization and everyone should become involved in implementing it. Therefore, conducting *awareness sessions* for everyone within the organization and how they will be involved in achieving them are critical.

Also, once the strategic plan is done, then a copy should be given to the departmental chairs so that they can, in turn, develop department goals based upon the overall school goals. The success of any strategic plan can never be achieved without proper monitoring and assessing its progress, step fifteen. Therefore, it is critical that a process for evaluating the goals is established, which might consist of periodic review meetings and conducting district-wide update sessions with everyone.

Step sixteen includes a review of the performance of individuals who are responsible for achieving the goals. This can be done through the performance appraisal process and periodic review meetings. Lastly, step seventeen includes an *evaluation of the strategic planning process* through extensive follow-up sessions by the original strategic plan members.

The evaluation might consist of *what things went well*, those *things that did not go well*, and *ideas for improving the process* in the strategic plan. Also, in monitoring the goals of a strategic plan, it can be helpful to develop a spreadsheet listing each of the major goals, the key strategies for each goal, who is responsible, target completion date, metrics, and status. In this way the goals can easily be reviewed, and comments can be written in the status section on the progress of each of the goals.

FORECASTING STUDENT ENROLLMENT

Human resource planning is an integral part of the strategic planning process and involves forecasting student enrollment for the school district, which helps administrators plan for future finances, and human resources. Forecasting student enrollment is like looking into a crystal ball, but not having 100 percent accuracy. It is an attempt to make the best educated guess based on analysis and available data.

Administrators can use several methods to help predict student enrollment, such as quantitative statistical analysis and qualitative techniques. Quantitative statistics involve calculating the number of children in an elementary school district and determining the number likely to enroll in high school. Specific trends in elementary school enrollment over two- to four-year periods of time can be used to help predict enrollment trends. It involves using analytics based on specific census data. In addition, feedback from local realtors and statistics from the planning commissions of local municipalities can provide statistics on housing trends and residency.

Qualitative measures consists of administrators using inductive analysis to make conclusions based upon discussions with people through the local chamber of commerce, identifying potential new businesses coming or leaving the area, residential and commercial developments that are being planned, the general economy in the area, and geographical potential for expansion. It relies heavily on past enrollment and trends to make judgments on future enrollments. For example, some school districts may be within a community that is landlocked or has older residents with decreasing numbers of children in school.

Also, new emerging communities that have high growth and new residential and commercial developments can provide valuable clues as to the direction of enrollment trends. However all this information must be perceived with caution in that a community may be rapidly growing but suddenly, due to economic reasons, the development can come to a halt, leaving school buildings empty and future plans for school expansion dormant.

The human resource planning strategy essentially involves matching the school's human resource needs with the projected student enrollment. Administrators must make a good-faith effort in determining this match in order to avoid shortages of teachers, overstaffing issues, or employing teachers who are the wrong people with the wrong certifications needed for the students. For example, if a community is experiencing a high growth in foreign immigrants, the necessity for bilingual and ESL programs may be more critical than other areas.

Likewise, nothing may be worse for an administrator than to overstaff a district and then experience a drastic decline in enrollment. This may necessitate a *reduction in force*. Recent legislation regarding desegregation and affirmative action has supported other means than using seniority as the basis whenever possible.

SUCCESSION PLANNING

Succession planning is a common practice in identifying and securing internal and external people to fill key administrative leadership positions within the organization. This process can be one of the most valuable ways to ensure that human resource needs are met. Generally succession planning, or sometimes called replacement planning, is used for identifying successors for key administrative and staff positions.

Oliver Wendall Holmes once stated that "the great thing in this world is not so much where we stand as in what direction we are going." The whole essence of succession planning is to be able to look into the future and ascertain which key positions need to be replaced. The succession planning process ensures that there is a successful transition of a candidate for a key position for the eventual retirement or unexpected separation of the incumbent from the position.

More simply stated, having a viable succession plan in place in the event of an unfortunate or abrupt departure of a key person can help weather the transition period, maintain operational continuity, and ensure the successful selection of a replacement in a timely manner. Moreover, it is good business sense to be well prepared for needed transitions in key management as well as all human resources.

Generally it is important that the superintendent of the school district establish a succession plan working with the school board. There needs to be a culture of honesty, trust, and mutual respect among members, because inherent conflicts and misunderstanding are natural during this process. Therefore the necessity of self-examination, critical analysis of current performance, spirited discussions, and candidness are hallmarks in balancing the multiplicity of viewpoints that can commonly occur.

The succession plan should be an ongoing and dynamic process that is regularly updated. It isn't something that should be viewed as a one-time exercise. The process can also serve as a useful process for self-examination, assessment of organizational current and future needs, and continuous improvement. It should be a thoughtful activity that serves the organization and ensures continuous improvement.

The succession planning process often begins by identifying possible candidates for selected positions to be filled. It is important to determine the future needs of the organization and having the end in sight versus focusing on past needs. Administrators who work collectively with an incumbent are more likely to establish a successful plan that is right for the future needs of the organization.

In other words, if a key person is replaced, the dynamics of the administrative team may be impacted due to the varying skill sets that all the team members and the incumbent have. Some typical questions for thoughtful reflection include:

- Is there an up-to-date job description and set of core competencies for the position?
- What are the mutual expectations of the school board and administrative leadership team?
- What are the major responsibilities for an ideal person in this position (versus the current job responsibilities of the position that might have evolved based upon the skills and talents of the incumbent, existing administrative team members, political dynamics, and organizational needs)?
- Who could be an immediate interim leader, and has he or she been notified in the event of an incumbent's departure?
- Has a key administrator been identified who could manage the transition during the time before replacing the incumbent?
- Has a developmental plan been initiated to help prepare the interim leader for the position?
- Have all potential issues been identified that need to be stabilized during the transition period upon an incumbent's abrupt departure that will ensure operational continuity?

Once there has been thoughtful analysis for the succession planning, the activity should start with completing a thorough process. The steps for the succession planning process are described as follows:

1. Develop a current job description for the incumbent position

   - Organizational role
   - Essential duties and responsibilities
   - Qualifications and requirements
   - Desired certificates, licenses, or registrations

2. Identify core competencies (skills, knowledge, and dispositions)

   - Leadership and administrative skills
   - Functional and technical skills

3. Determine board expectations
4. Identify and assess candidates for the incumbent's position
5. Provide development plan for internal candidates
6. Identify promotability of internal candidates (determine anticipated time frame)

The first step involves ensuring that a current *job description* is in place. The job description should be updated to include the organizational role; essential duties and responsibilities; qualifications and requirements; and desired certificates, licenses or registrations needed for the position. For example, a key position might be the business manager of a school district, principal, assistant superintendent for research and instructional development, or curriculum specialist.

The second step involves ensuring that the *core competencies*, which include performance skills, knowledge, and dispositions, have been developed for the key position. Generally these core competencies involve leadership and management skills as well as the actual functional/technical skills needed in the position. For example, if the core competencies for a position of an assistant superintendent or corporate vice president for research and instructional development were completed, there would be specific leadership and management skills needed to work with people as well as the technical expertise of understanding research and statistical analysis.

Step three involves working with the board to ensure that there is an agreed-upon *expectation* for the succession plan. Often a school board may work with an outside consultant to help facilitate the process and provide outside expertise and consultation.

Step four involves identifying and assessing *internal* and *external candidates* for the incumbent's position. Internal interim candidates should also be identified. This will help to ensure a smooth transition in the event of an abrupt departure of an incumbent.

Steps five includes identifying and providing a *developmental plan* for internal candidates for the position. The promotability of the candidate, step six, should be determined, along with an anticipated time frame from which the candidate could be ready to assume the position.

There are several core competencies that can be identified for a key administrative leadership position. While these core competencies may vary, many of them can be common for any leadership position. Described here is an example of a set of core competencies for an administrative leadership position.

1. *Strategic focus.* Is action-oriented, a visionary, proactive, anticipates the future, is innovative and energetic, and recognizes and seizes opportunities.
2. *Financial management.* Has good business acumen, competent financial abilities, budget management, resource planning, and reviews reports.
3. *Leadership skills.* Holds people accountable, delegates, mentors, makes good decisions, has composure, motivates staff and students, has courage, and is approachable.
4. *Teamwork.* Is collaborative, a motivator, trustworthy, fosters open dialogue, builds spirit and commitment to staff and students, and manages conflict.
5. *Communications.* Is a good listener; has good verbal, nonverbal, and written communication skills; has good presentation skills and meeting management skills.
6. *Student focus.* Has respect, understanding, and good sensitivity to all students.
7. *Ethics and integrity.* Conducts self with high ethics and integrity; adheres to school's values, beliefs, and mission; and understands essential school laws and policies.
8. *Instruction and curriculum.* Understands the critical aspects of instruction and curriculum.
9. *Problem-solving.* Solves difficult problems with effective solutions, has good analytical skills, forward thinker, and is a good decision-maker.
10. *Time management.* Demonstrates effective planning and organizing skills, can marshal resources (people, technology, materials) to get the job done.

11. *Technology expertise.* Is proficient in information technology, has experience with school software, and uses technology at a high rate of proficiency.
12. *Community resourcefulness.* Understands value and works with community and professional and business organizations in supporting the school.

When the set of core competencies has been completed, it is then important to identify potential candidates to replace the incumbent and to complete a checklist that can be filed and used when necessary. The core competencies can also serve as a basis of understanding the job responsibilities of a position. The checklist might also include the following items:

- Promotability—Is the candidate ready to assume the position now or how many years into the future?
- Gap analysis—The candidate should be evaluated based upon what specific gaps and core competencies are deficient and need to be developed.
- Career development plan—Once the gaps have been identified, then specific developmental actions should be completed for the candidate.
- Assigned mentor—An assigned mentor within the organization should also be responsible for completing the succession planning process and working with the candidates.

The journey in establishing an effective succession plan can be rewarding in many ways: promoting a robust discussion, building honesty and trust, reexamining expectations, assessing performance, brainstorming alternatives for organizational structure and initiatives, and identifying suitable candidates who can lead the school organization in the future. Ultimately, the end result should be a structured and viable succession plan that ensures operational continuity and promotes a diverse workplace.

EMPLOYMENT LAWS

The basis of human resource legalities is rooted in the United States Constitution. The *Bill of Rights* comprised the first set of amendments that were adopted and ratified by the United States Congress in 1789 (United States Bill of Rights, 2018). The purpose of this document was to enumerate the freedom given to all Americans, guarantee certain rights for citizens, and allow submission of grievances to the American government. Among this list of ten amendments, five of them have particular relevance to human resources.

The first amendment is the one that probably has the biggest relevance to human resources. This amendment states: "Congress shall make no law respecting an establishment of religion, or prohibiting the free exercise thereof; or abridging the freedom of speech, or of the press; or the right of the people peaceably to assemble, and to petition the Government for a redress of grievances" (United States Bill of Rights, 2018).

This amendment, in addition to allowing the right to practice religion, essentially provides the right to exercise *Freedom of Speech*. Americans have cherished this right of free expression. However, understanding exactly the full extent of this privilege, especially when it harms others, has been a subject of controversy. As a result, the extent and boundaries of free speech have been taken up by the U.S. courts numerous times with varying rulings.

There have been a myriad of questions surrounding the right of free speech, what constitutes the limitations, and when free speech crosses the line into criminal offenses against others. For example, some of these associated criminal offenses include libel, defamation, slander, threats of violence, harassment, obscenity, and hate crimes. For some people, defaming others, under the guise of freedom of speech, can be a convenient weapon to cause harm to other people.

The use of social media has served to test the legalities of free speech. The courts continue to sort out when people have an inherent right to their speech and when their speech and conduct violate others' rights. For example, should school teachers be allowed to voice their negative opinions about their organization when they are employed by the organization? Likewise, should students or employees have the right to use social media to post defamatory statements about their teachers or employers?

Another constitutional amendment that has significance to human resources is the fourth amendment. This amendment states: "The right of the people to be secure in their persons, houses, papers, and effects against unreasonable searches and seizures shall not be violated, and no warrants shall issue but upon probable cause, supported by oath or affirmation, and particularly describing the place to be searched and the persons or things to be seized" (United States Bill of Rights, 2018).

The fourth amendment protects people from unreasonable and warrantless searches by government, school districts, and other agencies into their personal information. However, how much confidentiality and reasonable considerations of noninvestigatory actions can be unclear. The extent to which a person's private locker at school can be searched or electronic information can be monitored and obtained under the interests of national security and then subsequently used against the person can be ambiguous. What are the powers and limits of the National Security Agency in monitoring and accessing a citizen's personal information?

Does the school district have the right to monitor and seize the personal information of students and staff? Likewise, do students or teachers have the right to prevent the intrusion by school or company authorities from using this personal information and taking punitive action against them? What are the boundaries that separate work-related actions and nonwork actions? Do people have the right of confidentiality, or is all personal information fair game for employers and officials when used on the Internet?

While the first and fourth amendments have the great significance to social media, the seventh, ninth, and tenth amendments have relevance as well. The seventh amendment provides "common law" rights to people involved in civil suits and jury protections, the ninth amendment ensures that certain rights shall not be construed to deny or disparage others by the people, and the tenth amendment ensures that powers not granted by the U.S. government are reserved by the states. All these amendments afford students and employees basic inherent rights of protection and due process.

Some of the federal and state laws and executive orders that have emerged from the initial Bill of Rights directly impact human resource employment. These laws cover a wide range of employment practices ranging from planning human resources to recruiting, interviewing, and selection; writing job descriptions; compensation; placement and induction; career development; mentoring practices; professional development; employee evaluation; collective bargaining; managing conflict; handling grievances; and termination and reduction in force (see table 1.1).

While there are many federal laws impacting education, there are also specific laws unique to individual states and school district policies. While federal laws tend to trump state and local laws, all of these laws must be understood and practiced by administrators. State laws and regulations generally specify certification and licensing regulations. Also, there are other regulation agencies like the state labor relations boards that impact school district policies.

Local school boards may establish higher standards than state regulations but generally cannot legally establish lower standards. An administrator must be well informed and seek local counsel in understanding the interrelationship of federal, state, and local school board laws and regulations.

For example, school boards may have the authority to set policy as long as the policy does not conflict with state laws. Also, there may be state laws that are not clearly defined by federal laws and statutes. For example, the State of Illinois added an anti-sexual orientation discrimination to the *Illinois Human Rights Act*.

Essentially this act states that it is unlawful to discriminate against sexual orientation as "actual or perceived heterosexuality, homosexuality, bisexuality or general related identity, whether or not traditionally associated with the person's designated sex at birth" (Illinois Department of Human Rights, 2018). These laws have reflected, in part, the changing values and feelings of society regarding equality and sexual orientation.

Table 1.1.   Major federal and EEOC laws and executive orders

Law	Basic Description
Title VII, Civil Rights Act of 1964 as amended	Prohibits discrimination on the basis of race, color, religion, national origin, gender, pregnancy, childbirth, and retaliation.
Equal Pay Act of 1963	Prohibits pay discrimination against males and females who perform equal work that is substantially the same.
1970 Occupational Safety and Health Act	Enforces standards for workplace safety and health to prevent work injuries, illnesses, and death (and regulations for safe work).
Title IV of the Education Amendments of 1972	Prohibits discrimination against males and females in activities and programs receiving federal funding and grants.
Rehabilitation Act of 1973 sections 501 & 505	Prohibits discrimination against qualified disabled people who can perform the major functions of a job and affirmative actions.
Vietnam Era Veterans' Readjustment Act of 1974	Requires employers with federal contracts to provide affirmative action for Vietnam era veterans to prevent discrimination.
Pregnancy Discrimination Act of 1978	Provides equal employment opportunity protection for pregnant women and new mothers that they be treated like any other disability for employment.
Family and Medical Leave Act of 1993	Requires employers to provide male and female employees up to twelve weeks a year in unpaid leave for qualified medical and family illness, military situations, pregnancy, foster care and adoption, or personal serious illness.
Title VII, Section 1604, Sexual Harassment Act	Prohibits unwelcome sexual advances, requests for sexual favors, and other verbal or physical conduct of a sexual nature that creates a hostile or offensive work environment.
1967 Age Discrimination Employment Act	Protects people who are forty or older from age discrimination or retaliation for filing a complaint.
1990 Title I Americans with Disabilities Act	Protects disabled people from employment discrimination or retaliation for filing a complaint.

Source: U.S. EEOC, www.eeoc.gov/laws, 2011.

This addition to the Human Rights Act has created controversy within many public schools and local school board opinions regarding sexuality and employment practices within a school district. State laws may also provide different employment work and compensation safeguards for teachers and staff. State and federal laws often work hand in hand and support each other. However, differences can exist.

For example, some states forbid school districts from waiving their rights granted by state law in matters concerning housing, compensation, cost of living adjustments, and contractual placement of teachers. Understanding the many federal and state laws is critical to reduce potential legal vulnerability for the school district, distress, and financial burden. However, some differences in state and federal law enforcement can exist such as in the case of immigration matters and political parties.

Many of the federal laws have originated based upon societal movements. During the late 1800s there were little federal laws that protected employees in the workplace. However, the *Human Relations Era* began in the 1930s that strongly influenced the passage of several federal legislative acts.

For example, in 1935 the *National Labor Relations Act* was established to prohibit discrimination against union members and employment and apprenticeship practices. There have been many additions to the Fair Labor Standards Act since 1938. Many of these provisions relate to child labor law, minimum wage requirements, overtime provisions, meals and breaks, travel, and training, as well as additional guidelines for exempt employees.

The *Labor Management Relations Act* was established in 1947. This Act, which is also known as the *Taft-Hartley Act*, was significant in outlining specific employment practices. This Act was an off-shoot to the original *National Labor Relations Act* and contains additional provisions and guidelines regarding employees' right to free speech and collection of union dues. Also during this time the *Federal Mediation Conciliation Service* was established to help resolve management and union disagreements.

EQUAL EMPLOYMENT OPPORTUNITY COMMISSION

As an outgrowth of the civil rights movement of the 1960s, the *Equal Employment Opportunity Commission* (EEOC) was established by *Title VII of the 1964 Civil Rights Act*. The original Act prohibited discrimination on the basis of race, color, relation, national origin, and gender. This law covered all aspects of employment including planning, hiring, supervising, compensation, job classification, promotions, training, and retirement and termination.

While the *Civil Rights Act* primarily covered all employers and public and private institutions with fifteen or more employees, the Act provided the basis for bringing litigation against institutions that practiced discriminatory acts. This federal law created protected classes of employees that mainly consisted of women, African Americans, Asians, Hispanics, Indians, and Eskimos.

Subsequently, amendments have been made to the Act, which included protecting individuals above age forty, disabled people, and pregnant women. Also, in 1978, the EEOC adopted other guidelines to protect claims of reverse discrimination practices as an outgrowth of affirmative action. Essentially, the act stated that organizations should avoid selection policies that have an adverse impact on hiring or employment opportunities because of race, gender, or ethnicity unless there is an organizational necessity for the practice.

The penalties associated with *Civil Rights Act* violations can be severe. The law allows individuals who have been discriminated against to seek compensatory and punitive damages for both willful and intentional discrimination acts. Compensatory damages generally involve harm to an employee that induces pain and emotional suffering.

Punitive damages can be assessed against an employer, which serves as punishment and a deterrent for others. There are some limitations for judgment awards depending upon the size of an organization. In addition to the EEOC, violations of discrimination are also enforced, and judgments can be awarded by state human rights commissions. For example, the State of Illinois has a *Department of Human Rights Commission*, which is responsible for protecting individuals from discriminatory practices.

Both the EEOC and state human rights commissions have the authority to assess monetary penalties, and both of these agencies have established time frames in which a claim can be filed. For example, the State of Illinois typically allows for 180 days from the occurrence, and the EEOC allows 300 days. Not only can an organization incur financial costs for acts of discrimination, but they can also incur significant emotional pain, legal costs, work disruption, and wasted time and resources defending claims. Therefore, organizations are wise to follow legal practices and avoid claims of discrimination.

The *Equal Pay Act of 1963* was an outgrowth to the Fair Labor Standards Act. This law prohibits compensation discrimination for people who have the same skills and experiences and are performing the same job. However, there can be several exceptions to pay differences such as bonuses for higher performances, seniority, merit, working conditions, geographic differences, and quality and quantity of work. The law primarily serves to protect differences in pay between men and women who are substantially doing the same work and have the same qualifications, performance, and seniority.

The Occupational Safety and Health Act (OSHA) was established in 1970. This Act included mandatory safety and health standards for all employers. The objective of the Act is to prevent occupational injuries and illnesses by enforcing standards of workplace safe practices. The law is enforced by the OSHA agency, a division of the *United States Department of Labor*.

This agency, in addition to implementing investigations for work-related injuries, also initiates proactive inspections to organizations when there is a possible hazard or danger to people. This law has had a major impact on school district facilities and requires administrators to ensure that the facilities are safe and do not impose health risks and illnesses to staff and students.

The agency has the power to impose monetary fines and requires facility improvements. The agency also provides significant safety regulations involving permissible exposure limits, personal protective equipment, hazard communications, safety management, blood-borne pathogens, evacuations, exposure to asbestos, and in some cases, mandatory training for safety and health practices.

Title IV of the Education Amendments Act of 1972 prohibits discrimination on the basis of gender for educational programs by recipients of federal financial assistance. The Act states: "No persons in the United States shall, on the basis of sex, be excluded from participating in, be denied the benefits of, or be subjected to discrimination under any program or activity receiving Federal financial assistance" (U.S. Equal Employment Opportunity Commission, 2018).

This law requires school districts to maintain internal procedures for federal grants and resolving complaints of discrimination. In addition, Title IV also applies to programs of a school district regardless of whether the program is federally funded. This law outlines specific guidelines that school districts need to follow to maintain compliance.

The Rehabilitation Act of 1973 serves to promote equality for employees with disabilities. This law requires that employers take affirmative action to recruit, hire, and promote qualified, disabled people. The law serves to protect disabled persons who can perform the main functions of the job with reasonable accommodations. While the law has good intentions, some administrators may have difficulty interpreting exactly what "reasonable accommodations" means.

The law does not mandate that accommodations be made if it imposes a significant hardship or monetary expense that is unreasonable for a school district. However, in most cases administrators can accommodate disabled employees through actions such as modifying work schedules, providing ergonomic devices, and providing other special equipment or modifications to support a disabled person in performing the primary functions of a job.

Examples of accommodations might include installing entrance ramps for people in wheelchairs, special seat cushions for back pathologies, wrist splints for accumulative trauma disorders, and special lighting for people with eye-related diseases. It should be noted that a school district is not required to hire a disabled person who is less qualified than nondisabled people. The intention of the law is to prevent discrimination against disabled people who can perform the major functions of the job.

The Vietnam Era Veterans' Readjustment Act of 1974 followed the Vietnam War. This Act mandates that employers take affirmative action to recruit, hire, and promote Vietnam War veterans and disabled veterans. Definitions of veterans of the Vietnam War include U.S. military, ground, naval, or air service people who served during the period of 1964 through 1975. The regulations of the law are intended to prevent employers from discriminating against protected Vietnam War veterans.

This law mainly impacts contractors or subcontractors receiving federal funds. In addition, employers are required to keep records for at least two years. However employers who have less than 150 employees are required to maintain records for only one year. Examples of records include job descriptions, job advertisements, interview notes, applications, resumes, employment policies, human resource files, and any related employment forms and records.

The *Pregnancy Discrimination Act of 1978* provides protection for pregnant women and new mothers that they be treated like another disability for employment matters. This act was an amendment to the Title VII of Civil Right Act and impacts organizations with at least fifteen employees. This law would provide protection for pregnant women in hiring, promotion, and terminating practices.

The *Family and Medical Leave Act of 1993* (FMLA) prohibits discrimination to male and female employees who desire to take twelve weeks of unpaid leave because of the birth of a child, adoption or foster care of a child, or caring for a family member who has a serious health condition. This law is administered by the *Wage and Hour Division* of the United States Department of Labor.

The law supports people who have qualified medical and family situations leaving decisions to the discretion of the employer. Interpretation of the law is not always clear-cut, and while guidelines have been provided by the federal agency, questions regarding what medical situations qualify remain. Local attorney counsel is advised when administering actions based on federal laws to ensure proper compliance.

For example, the federal FMLA does not recognize many part-time workers who desire unpaid leave, or certain employers with less than 50 employees. Also, employees who desire to take unpaid time off for illnesses of relatives, pets, personal short-term illness, or other routine medical care are generally excluded. It is generally a good policy to try and work with employees during these times to maintain job satisfaction and morale.

Other related FMLA state statutes may apply as well. For example, the State of California recognizes domestic partners and children of domestic partners. Connecticut, on the other hand, recognizes parent-in-laws of civil union partners, and the State of Hawaii recognizes grandparents of employees.

The EEOC included a sexual harassment amendment in 1980 to the Title VII of Civil Rights Act. This law prohibits *sexual harassment* in the workplace. The law states that sexual harassment involves "Unwelcome sexual advances, requests for sexual favors, and other verbal or physical conduct of a sexual nature—when such conduct has the purpose or effect of unreasonably interfering with an individual's work performance or creating an intimidating, hostile or offensive working environment" (U.S. Equal Employment Opportunity Commission, 2018).

There are several types of sexual harassment discrimination in this amendment. *Adverse impact discrimination* involves the unintentional actions that have negative or detrimental effects against a person or group of people. This discrimination might involve requiring certain height requirements that could unintentionally discriminate against people of a certain ethnicity. *Adverse treatment discrimination* involves the intentional act of treating people differently.

An example of this discrimination could be asking different interview questions for men versus women during an employment interview. *Retaliation* is an intentional discrimination when an employer commits an adverse action against the employee because he or she has complained against discrimination or filed a discrimination claim. Another type of sexual discrimination is called *quid pro quo*. This harassment (or called this for that) (in exchange for) requests sexual favors in exchange for some type of employment benefit.

An example of quid pro quo might be a school administrator requesting sexual favors from a teacher in exchange for a good performance rating or promotion. A type of sexual harassment discrimination that amounts to *environmental sexual harassment* is called *hostile working environment*. Essentially the law can be described as "I can't take it anymore," which often is the way people feel in this type of work environment.

This type of harassment involves any unreasonable actions that interfere with an employee's work performance that have a sexual basis. Examples might include verbal, physical, and visual sexual actions; patently offensive conduct; harassment of individuals because of their gender; displaying inappropriate sexual pictures; physically touching people; or sending sexually based content e-mails.

Sexual harassment complaints have significantly increased over the past years. School administrators are required to post sexual harassment policies, conduct investigations when complaints have been received, take action against offenders, provide training for employees, and provide an employee complaint mechanism or grievance system. Many state laws have similar provisions to the Federal Title VII amendment. Sexual harassment discrimination has become a complex law and requires school administrators to consult legal counsel.

The *Age Discrimination in Employment Act of 1967* was designed to prohibit age discrimination for employees over forty years of age in planning, recruiting, selection, training, promoting, transferring, compensating, and other practices of employment. The intention of the law is to prevent companies from discharging or refusing to hire older workers based upon their age.

In 1986 this act was amended to prohibit discrimination in retirement for people above forty years of age. An example of this law would include a school district that forced a competent sixty-year-old teacher to retire against his or her will in order to hire a twenty-two-year-old teacher in order to save money for the school district. It should be noted that this law protects people who are forty years of age or older but does not protect people who are under the age of forty.

It is never a good practice to hire or fire people based upon age rather than performance factors and needs of the school. Also, because of this law many school districts have offered early retirement programs in an effort to encourage retirement and reduce costs. It is often difficult for organizations to try and balance good intentions in accommodating students and employees and the financial budgets.

The *Americans with Disabilities Act of 1990 Title I* was established to prevent discrimination against disabled individuals who can perform the essential functions of a job with reasonable accommodations. This law generally applies to employers who have fifty or more employees. This law has had significant impact on school districts given that it covers such a wide range of medical conditions such as HIV, mental illnesses, learning disabilities, alcohol and drug addiction, and other physical ailments.

This law is executed under the Equal Employment Opportunity Commission and was subsequently amended to prohibit school districts from discrimination regardless of the number of employees. This law has been controversial in regard to the extent in which organizations try to balance the needs of disabled people and the financial needs of the organization and productivity in serving students and customers.

Some more recent state laws address the actions of *bullying* and *stalking*. Many states have adopted anti-bullying and stalking-stalking laws. The hurt and emotional harm that can be done by these actions can have long-lasting impact to victims. Some examples of these actions include posting unauthorized pictures and videos of students, abusive comments, hacking or fraudulently executing posts through other names and venues, and making intimidating and threatening statements.

People can become victims of harassment by face-to-face contact or through the Internet. Federal and state laws provide protection to people from harassment, which generally includes obscene comments with the intent of offending, threatening, or creating a hostile environment to others. In addition to harassment, extortion and stealing of nonconsensual material by a perpetrator's interception may constitute criminal and civil liability. These actions may also violate federal interstate commerce laws. Severe penalties can be given to these offenders.

Another common criminal act is the case of *defamation* of school educators, staff, and other students. Using hate blogs or websites or Twitter to defame others can result in severe penalties and civil action. Defamation is not reserved to only newspapers, radio, or television but can be done through any type of communication media. And it doesn't matter how many people are exposed to the defamation.

A serious issue that impacts social media is the posting of *threats* against other people or an organization. The courts have wrestled with what social media postings constitute a viable threat. Students who make open threats that reasonably can be construed as legitimate run the risk of being prosecuted. Moreover, *threats of violence* and shootings must be taken seriously and investigated.

The best policy to take in using social media is to treat each other with respect and dignity. All social media users should review and understand organizational policies, local community ordinances, and state and federal laws governing social media actions and conduct. The temptation to violate these policies and laws may come with severe penalties and damage, not only to others but also to the perpetrators themselves.

SUMMARY

The primary goal of human resource planning is to forecast the future needs of an organization and to ensure that all resources are obtained. Proper planning entails understanding the goals of the organization, anticipating changes in staffing, understanding and staying current with federal and state laws and local district policies, and working with school administrators to match current organizational resources and current needs with future resources and future needs.

There are many strategies used to help plan and predict resources such as strategic planning, succession planning, and human resource forecasting to satisfy future organizational needs, financial facilities, and human resource needs. Proper planning allows for all administrators to develop a framework to recruit, select, hire, mentor, and develop people to meet future staffing needs. There is no one strategy that can guarantee a perfect prediction of all human resource needs, since the planning process is a dynamic one and must adapt to the changing needs of the organization.

Therefore, the human resource planning process is matching the needs of a school with available people. The bottom-line is that "the trains must leave on time," and all operations and staffing need to be in place to best service the educational needs of the students.

CASE STUDY

Washington Magnet School—
Creating a Ninety-Day Entry Plan

Washington School is a magnet school in an urban environment serving about 1,600 students from early childhood to eighth grade. The school specializes in the language arts and is recognized throughout the city as being a good academic institution. The school is searching for a new principal since the recent termination of the last principal for poor performance.

There is a myriad of problems at the school which include:

1. Low test scores.
2. Low staff morale.
3. High attrition rate of teachers.
4. Frequent complaints from parents regarding curriculum, instruction, and school policies.
5. Several recent filings of sexual harassment complaints against male teachers by female teachers.
6. A lack of financial accountability and controls.

In addition to these issues the district has made several recent policy changes that have impacted the school. These policies will increase the student enrollment at the school over the next two years. This increase in students will put a strain on the school's capacity, and there will be a need to expand the facilities of the school in order to accommodate this increased enrollment. Also, additional staff must be hired to accommodate these new students.

The school board is in the process of hiring a new principal who could start immediately to address these issues and plan for the future. You are a candidate for the principal position, and the school board has asked you to prepare "a ninety-day entry plan" outlining what you would do as a new principal during your first ninety days on the job.

The school board would like for you to prepare this written, comprehensive ninety-day entry plan and present it at the next board meeting. This should include detailed human resource planning, communication, facilities, legal concerns, staff morale, budget and finance, instruction and curriculum, enrollment projection, and any other factors deemed important.

Exercises and Discussion Questions

1. Develop a comprehensive strategic plan for your school following the steps outlined in this chapter.
2. Using your school as an example, prepare a succession plan for the assistant principal position.
3. Interview a school administrator and outline the process for human resource planning that is being used.
4. Interview a school administrator and identify some of the major legal issues confronting the school including recent complaints and lawsuits.
5. List and describe at least six different EEOC laws or executive orders.
6. Outline the grievance or complaint procedure for a staff member to follow in filing a sexual harassment claim at the school.
7. Explain the history and process of the EEOC.
8. List and explain the laws that protect people on the basis of race, sex, religion, national origin, age, and disability.
9. Research and list some laws unique to your state and how they support federal laws.

REFERENCES

Illinois Department of Human Rights. (2018). State of Illinois, US/dhr.

United States Bill of Rights. (2018). https://www.loc.gov/rr/program/bib/ourdocs/billofrights.html.

United States Equal Employment Opportunity Commission. (2018). www.eeoc.gov/laws.

Chapter 2

Recruitment and Selection

Objectives

At the conclusion of this chapter you will be able to:

1. Understand recruitment strategies and procedures used by corporate managers and school administrators (ELCC 3.1, PSEL 3).
2. Differentiate between federal and state laws that impact recruitment and employment practices (ELCC 6.1, 6.2, 6.3, PSEL 6).
3. Understand reasons why candidates select an organization for employment (ELCC 3.1, PSEL 3).
4. Describe the typical selection process used by school districts (ELCC 3.1, 3.3, PSEL 3).
5. Understand different interviewing techniques used for selecting the best candidates for positions (ELCC 2.1, 3.3, PSEL 3).

RECRUITING APPLICANTS

Human resource recruiting is a critical part of the job of the organizational leader. Recruiting the best candidates to fill job positions is a dynamic process and a never-ending one. Throughout the decades the United States school districts have experienced dramatic shifts in student enrollment. For example, in the 1960s, the student population significantly increased and then began a gradual decline during the 1970s, reflecting the changing population age in the United States.

Although the United States experienced a recession in 2008, most public school districts continued to employ large numbers of teachers largely because of increased federal stimulus funding. In the 2018 school year over 50 million students were attending public elementary and secondary schools. Over 35 million of these students were enrolled in prekindergarten through eighth grade and about 5 million were enrolled in high school. Another 6 million students were enrolled in private schools (National Center for Education Statistics, 2018).

Without a doubt education is a big business. It is estimated that public school districts will hire over 3 million teachers in 2018. This represents a student-teacher ratio of 15.5. This ratio compares to a student-teacher ratio of 16.0 in the year 2000. Private schools are experiencing significantly lower teacher-to-student ratios. For example, in the fall of 2018 the National Center for Education Statistics estimated that the private school student-teacher ratio was 12.9, which represents a significantly lower ratio than in public education (National Center for Education Statistics, 2018).

Also, attendance in college has been increasing as well. According to the National Center for Education statistics, the total enrollment in postsecondary degree-granting institutions is expected to increase 15 percent between fall 2010 and fall 2021. The agency describes postsecondary institutions as degree-granting schools that provide study beyond secondary school and offer programs terminating in an associate's, baccalaureate, or higher degree and participate in federal financial aid programs (National Center for Education Statistics, 2018).

Although there have been increases in the teacher employment, school districts vary from one another in the number of teachers being hired. Many school districts are experiencing financial difficulties and are not recruiting or hiring many, if any, teachers. Much of the fiscal condition of a school district and subsequent hiring practices are impacted by the amount of local community tax and state funding.

Also, some teachers who planned for early retirement have prolonged their retirement given the economic downturn and need to support family or maintain a desired standard of living. For example, during the 1980s, large number of teachers retired and created many vacancies for new recruits. During the recession of 2008 and subsequent years, there have been fewer retirements, which have caused a decrease in the hiring of new teachers. The increase in students is creating added demands for additional teacher and staff for both public and private educational institutions.

The recruitment process of teachers and staff is a proactive one. Administrators need to predict job vacancies and fill them with the intention of securing long-term employees. The recruitment process is also expensive for a school district, and hiring the wrong teachers only serves to increase these costs as well as contribute to lower morale and operating inefficiencies. Therefore, school administrators need to take the recruitment process very seriously and strive to select the best candidates for their school district. Likewise, applying for job vacancies can be a very competitive and time-consuming process for applicants.

If an applicant is not selected for an interview or for employment, he or she may feel that there was discrimination involved and can react by filing a complaint or lawsuit against the school district. Therefore, administrators need to practice all safeguards to ensure that the recruiting process is professional and compliant with all federal, state, and district laws and policies.

There are many reasons why applicants apply for a school other than compensation. Sometimes people may assume that the main purpose for a teacher applying to a school is pay and benefits. However, this is not always the case. People are motivated to work for both extrinsic and intrinsic reasons. Described here are typical reasons why applicants select a school:

1. Close proximity of school to home.
2. Geographic location.
3. Working environment.
4. Academic reputation of school.
5. Supportive administrators.
6. Compensation and benefits.
7. Promotion and growth opportunities.
8. Personal identity with school.
9. Specialization of the school.
10. Religious affiliation of a private school.
11. Culture at the school.
12. Desirable working hours.
13. Types of educational programs.

Extrinsic factors are tangible items such as pay, benefits, work conditions, and supervision practices. Intrinsic factors are intangible things such as appreciating the academic mission of the school, feeling connected with the school, interesting work, receiving full appreciation for work, and the love for the actual work itself.

These factors can vary from one school to another. A private school with a strong religious culture can attract applicants for employment if they value this environment. However, an applicant might be motivated to work at an urban school with poor working conditions and high disciplinary problems if there is good compensation and they value money as a major priority.

Some people are more motivated by money rather than other factors. Some applicants may be partial toward the diversity and ethnicity of the school student population. Also, a school that has a largely Hispanic student population may attract applicants who are Hispanic. Understanding the driving forces that influence job seekers is always challenging. However, school human resources and employment agencies need to keep abreast of these reasons to remain competitive and obtain the best candidates.

Administrators need to be sensitive to the type of student population, ethnicity, and religious affiliation when recruiting the best qualified teachers for the school. Administrators need to understand the motivation of applicants and to have a realistic discussion with applicants to ensure that there is a good fit between the applicants and the school. From a finance standpoint, administrators need to recognize these intrinsic and extrinsic motivators when planning school budgets and negotiating compensation contracts.

The conceptual framework for the hiring process can be seen as having three distinct components: *recruiting*, *selecting*, and *orientating* (see figure 2.1). This process needs to be completed following all federal, state, and

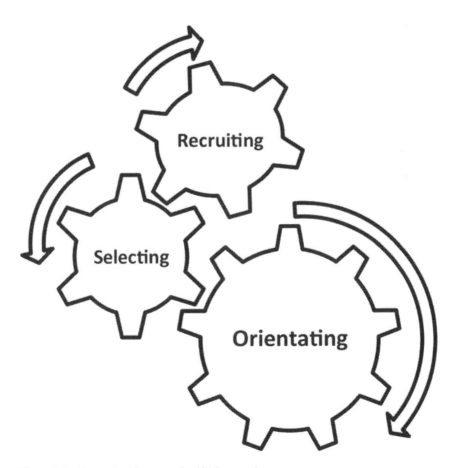

Figure 2.1. Conceptual framework of hiring employees.

local laws. The process starts with planning for recruitment. Described here are several steps for the recruitment planning process:

1. Develop strategic plan and organizational goals.
2. Create a process for position control and approval.
3. Forecast potential vacancies and budget.
4. Establish job analysis and certification requirements.
5. Develop job descriptions.
6. Obtain school board approval.
7. Post internal and external job openings.
8. Begin recruiting applicants.
9. Establish a pool of candidates.

The recruiting process begins with developing a comprehensive *strategic plan* that includes the goals of the school. These goals should determine the staffing needs for school. For example, if the goals are to promote English as a Second Language (ESL) and bilingual programs, then qualified applicants will need to be secured. Also, if the school is experiencing excessive student disciplinary problems, then a disciplinary dean position may need to be created.

There needs to be a process for posting positions, controlling the activity, and gaining approval for postings, interviews, and selection. Also, the job positions of a school should be based upon the anticipated educational and organizational needs of the school as determined by the school board. Once a position has been forecasted, a complete *job analysis* needs to be done. A job analysis outlines the knowledge, skills, dispositions, and tasks needed in the position. The job analysis is used as a foundation to create a job description.

A job description should clearly outline the duties and responsibilities of a position and should conform to the *Americans with Disabilities Act* (ADA) guidelines. The ADA requires that all job descriptions provide the necessary requirements for a position in order to understand the functions of the job for disabled applicants. A typical job description would contain topics such as:

1. Title of the position and whether exempt or nonexempt status.
2. Summary of the job description.
3. Essential duties and responsibilities.
4. Special qualification requirements.
5. Education and certification requirements.
6. Special skills required (language, mathematical reasoning ability, etc.).
7. Certificates, licenses, and registrations.
8. Physical demands.
9. Work environment conditions.

A *job description* needs to be thorough and complete. Applicants need to know the essential duties and responsibilities including the physical demands and conditions of the work environment. For example, an applicant should know how many pounds of weight he or she may be required to lift; amount of standing, sitting, or stooping; and hearing and visual qualities required for a job. All of this information is needed to meet ADA requirements. These requirements also serve as a basis for determining *reasonable accommodations* that are necessary to enable individuals with disabilities to perform the essential functions of the job.

For example, if an employee needs to work in outside weather conditions for extended periods of time or in dirty or noisy work environments, these requirements should be specific and clearly outlined. Every job is different. The job of a teacher in a classroom is going to be different than a building engineer or a groundskeeper. Maintaining current and accurate job descriptions is key to these situations.

For example, if a bus driver is being hired, he or she may need to have a valid commercial driver's license and acceptable peripheral and distance vision, which may be different for a teacher. If a building engineer needs to be able to occasionally lift 25 pounds, this essential job function needs to be clearly outlined in the physical demands section. If an applicant is unable, due to physical disability, to lift these amounts, then he or she may be rejected as an applicant.

Therefore, it is critical that administrators follow appropriate legal guidelines and seek legal counsel in administering the recruiting and selection process. Once the job descriptions have been completed and approved by the school board, the job openings can be posted. Some job openings might be first posted internally and then opened to the public. After posting the job openings, the recruiting process begins by creating a pool of candidates to interview.

There are many sources for recruiting teachers and staff. Although most organizations use an online recruitment and application system to screen applicants, described here is an array of typical employment recruiting sources:

1. Employee referrals
2. Electronic databases
3. Internet websites
4. District website
5. Job fairs
6. Employment agencies
7. Professional associations
8. Print media

9. Broadcast media
10. Educational institutions
11. Recruiting brochures
12. Unsolicited applicants and walk-ins

One of the best sources of potential applicants is *personal referrals* from employees. While some people may think that employees may be eager to recommend a friend or relative for a job, they may have second thoughts if the person is poorly qualified and they have to work with this person. Many people will not compromise their values and recommend a person unless they feel the applicant is highly qualified and is a good fit for the position and organization.

Referrals by employees are often desirable, since it is one of the least costly sources of recruiting. One of the best ways for applicants to be referred to a school for employment is to get to know the teachers and administrators at the school. This often can be done through participation in professional associations, student teaching assignments, and substitute teaching where they have an opportunity to get to work with these people.

In the corporate world sometimes employers are given a referral bonus for recommending people who are hired. This practice is not common in school institutions, but the referring employee may receive intangible rewards through recognition and satisfaction of recommending qualified applicants. Many school districts have also established policies and procedures regarding nepotism and referring of applicants for potential candidates.

The advent of technology has dramatically changed the recruiting process. The use of electronic databases, Internet, and the school district websites are all very quick, convenient, and efficient sources for recruiting applicants. There are numerous job websites that can be utilized, such as websites of educational associations, universities, employment search firms, and State Department of Education.

Other recruiting sources can range from attending job fairs to using employment agencies. The use of *employment agencies*, often called head-hunters, is largely reserved for securing upper-level administrators. Use of employments agencies can be costly to the school district and can range from 10 percent to 30 percent of the employee's first-year salary. Some advantages to using employment agencies include a comprehensive screening of all applicants, extensive completion of background checks, and professional consultation. Search firms can also be beneficial when trying to obtain hard-to-find candidates for a position.

Print and *broadcast media* continue to be used still today, although to a lesser degree than websites. Advertisements can be placed in professional educational association print materials such as newsletters, magazines, and journals. Some educational organizations include the *Association for Supervision and Curriculum Development*, *National Association of Elementary School Principals*, *National Association of Secondary School Principals*, *National School Boards Association*, and the *American Association of School Personnel Administrators* (AASPA).

Some of these associations, such as *American Association of School Administrators* (AASPA), actually produce a job bulletin. This bulletin offers free job searching and resume posting. It offers a section exclusively for job seekers and allows them to view all jobs in the bulletin, and new jobs are posted every week. There is also a special section for employers and recruiters that can be utilized to post positions, although there is a fee for the use of this service.

Another inexpensive source is the *unsolicited application*. Virtually every school district receives unsolicited job inquiries. This source can be much cheaper than the expense of advertising and attending job fairs and conferences. However, depending upon the district, the number of inquiries and applications can be voluminous. If a popular school district has only a few openings, it is not unusual to receive literally thousands of applications. This can be overwhelming for the human resources administrator in tracking and responding to all of these inquiries. Nevertheless, this can be a very valuable source of identifying good applicants for a vacancy.

Human resources administrators need to become proficient in developing a system for screening these applications. Search committees are often formed to help screen the qualified applicants. Also, administrative assistants are used to sort through applications, screen the applications, and select the ones that meet the qualifications of a job. For example, recruitment expenses can range from advertisement costs, travel, meals and lodging, convention registration fees, and time for participating in these events.

The recruitment process is one that is a necessity for all school districts in securing the best qualified people to fulfill the needs of the organization. Following federal, state, and local district laws and policies is critical in ensuring that the recruiting process is compliant and nondiscriminatory. Administrators need to understand these laws and also seek legal counsel to ensure compliance with them.

All administrators involved in the recruiting process should periodically evaluate the recruitment program. This evaluation may include the use of efficient resources, time and effort, cost per employee hired, and quality of the database system. The goal is to incorporate a continuous improvement process that is efficient and cost-effective for recruiting best qualified applicants for the school.

The entire planning and management of human resources can be integrated into one computer system called *Enterprise Resource Planning* (ERP). The ERP is a computer system that integrates internal and external administrative functions of human resources, finance, accounting, and operations into one database. ERPs are excellent systems for employees to calculate human resource costs, provide real-time data access, file and track employee information, administrative record keeping, contractual agreements with unions, and business functions of the organization.

There are many screening tools and employment platforms that can be used by school districts. Most of these platforms offer user-friendly, Internet-based education management systems that provide a variety of functions and support such as live chat, phone, and e-mail. Also, the systems tend to be data-driven and offer functions such as:

1. Holistic tracking and reporting of recruiting process and candidates.
2. Interview packages that allow the interviewing team to learn interviewing strategies and provide feedback.
3. Alert and tracking features to optimize performance and the interview process.
4. Automated functions of scheduling, collecting, and interviewing feedback.
5. Interactive communications systems for employers and candidates.
6. Additional features of instruction and curriculum and student reporting data.

Several of the systems are also available as cloud-based PK–12 school administrative software solutions. These systems can provide efficiency and money. They also provide ancillary features such as management of attendance, gradebooks, textbooks, scheduling, report cards, invoicing, discipline, accounting and finance, budgeting, and mobile apps. In addition, some other features include cafeteria, resource management, health and medical care, admissions processes, and online applications and forms.

Examples of school management systems include Greenhouse, Skyward, Infinite Vision, Escape, Digital Schools, Newton, Orbund, Rediker, Gradelink, and SchoolMint. One system, called TADS Admissions and Enrollment, provides an integrated web-based tuition management, admission, enrollment, financial aid, and school management for private and public schools. Another system, called Edvance School-Wide Management System, is designed to provide a web-based student information system for managing activities such as admissions, workloads, scheduling, personalized learning, curriculum management, and parent portal and analytics.

SELECTING APPLICANTS

The goal of the selection process is to interview and select the best qualified applicant for a job position. Selecting a candidate can be a costly endeavor.

The process requires a number of activities such as planning, interviewing, screening, selecting, completing reference checks, and obtaining legal counsel. Therefore, school districts need to develop the most efficient selection process that is cost-effective and maximizes the use of internal resources, since there is often a tension between quality and cost (see figure 2.2).

The interviewing process, if done right, is a comprehensive one. Described here is a list of steps for the interviewing process:

 1. Gain approval for job position and establish budget.
 2. Establish a search committee.
 3. Review federal and state interviewing laws.
 4. Advertise job position.
 5. Screen applicants.
 6. Interview applicants.
 7. Select the best candidate for job position.
 8. Extend offer for employment.
 9. Conduct background and reference checks.
10. Finalize mutual acceptance and documentation.

Much of the work for the interview takes place before and after the interview session. There can be an enormous amount of time and effort in the planning process alone. The process begins with the formation of a selection committee. This group may consist of the human resources administrator, school principal, and selected teachers or staff. Some administrators may feel that more participation adds to a more quality selection process and the more likely all the employees will be inclined to accept the new employees.

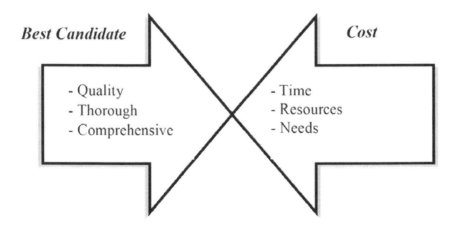

Figure 2.2. Tension of selecting best candidate and cost.

Besides the search committee, sometimes stakeholders are involved in the selection process. The school board often approves vacancies and positions, and the central office administrators are generally responsible for the overall process. Also, teacher unions may have contractual agreements that impact the selection process.

The overall objective is to hire the best candidate for a position and to obtain employment longevity. The process fails when the wrong applicant is hired for a position or separates from the organization within a short amount of time. Once the selection committee has been formed, the members need to understand all preemployment legal guidelines and review the application form, electronic databases, resumes, job requirements, and other materials for undertaking the screening and interview process. Once the job description has been advertised, then applicants are generally required to complete the job application. Figure 2.3 shows a typical job application.

Prior to scheduling the interview sessions, the members of the screening committee need to thoroughly understand all the preemployment laws that impact interviewing a candidate). The members need to understand permissible and nonpermissible questions for the interviewing process (see table 2.1). For example, many unacceptable applications list questions that are contrary to federal and state laws.

It is generally unacceptable to ask a person's age and date of graduation from a school on the application form. These types of questions may violate federal, state, and EEOC laws, since they may reveal a person's age and constitute age discrimination. Questions regarding if an applicant has been arrested are generally unacceptable. Some legal experts feel that there have been a disproportionate number of arrests of minorities in the United States.

Therefore, if a school district were to use the number of arrests versus the number of convictions, they could be inadvertently discriminating against minority applicants, which may violate the Civil Rights Act. However, questions regarding if an applicant has been convicted of a crime are generally appropriate, especially when the nature of the business involves students. School administrators have a responsibility to keep the students safe and free from potential criminal acts.

Generally speaking, felony convictions involving sex, drugs, and physical violence would disqualify an applicant from employment. A teacher would also not be able to obtain a state teaching license if convicted of these types of crimes. The nature of the crime conviction needs to be relevant to the job of the applicant. For example, if an applicant is applying for a job as a groundskeeper and has been convicted of a felony of tax evasion, rejecting the applicant on this basis may be illegal.

However, if an applicant is applying for a business director position at a school district and he or she has had a prior felony conviction for tax evasion

SAMPLE APPLICATION FOR EMPLOYMENT
APPLICANTS MAY BE TESTED FOR ILLEGAL DRUGS

Date: _____

Name _____
    Last   First   Middle   Maiden

Present Address _____
    Number   Street   City   State   Zip

How Long? _____ Social Security No. _____

Telephone ( )   Are you 18 years or older?   Yes _____   No _____

Type of School	Name of School	Location (complete mailing address)	Number of Years Completed	Major/Degree & Certification
High School				
College				

Have you been convicted of a crime?   Yes _____   No _____   (please circle yes or no)
If yes, explain number of conviction(s), nature of offense(s) leading to conviction(s), how recently such offence(s) was/were committed, sentence(s) imposed, and type(s) of rehabilitation.

CURRENT EMPLOYER

Date Month and Year	Name and Address of Employer	Salary	Position	Reason for Leaving
From				
To				

FORMER EMPLOYERS (List Below Last Two Employers, Starting With Last One First)

Date Month and Year	Name and Address of Employer	Salary	Position	Reason for Leaving
From				
To				
From				
To				

REFERENCES

Name	Address	Phone	Years Acquainted

I certify the application information is true, and if I am employed I may be terminated if the information is found not true. I authorize the school district to investigate this information and check references, and I release the school district from all claims for obtaining such information. If hired, I will be an employee at will and can be terminated any time.

_____   _____
            Signature   Date

Figure 2.3. Sample application for employment.

Table 2.1. Acceptable and unacceptable preemployment questions

Subject	Acceptable	Unacceptable
Name	Have you used any other names?	Was your name changed by court order?
Residence	What is your address?	Do you own a home or have any foreign residences? How long have you lived at your residence?
Age	If hired, can you show proof of age? Are you over eighteen years of age?	Birthdate, age, dates of attendance, or date of completion of school, or questions that identify over age forty.
Birthplace, citizenship	After employment, submit verifications of your legal right to work in the United States.	Your birthplace, parents, or spouse. Are you a U.S. citizen? Or, do you have naturalization papers?
National origin	What languages do you read, speak, and write? Can you speak, read, or write Spanish?	What is your mother's native language? Where did you learn to speak your languages?
Sex,family	What is the name and address of your parent or guardian if you are a minor? What is your gender (if a BFOQ job)?	Questions about applicant's sex; marital status; children or dependents and childcare; or pregnancy, childbearing, or birth control.
Race,color	Can you provide a photograph after you are hired? (Personal data for federal governmental affirmative action.)	Questions as to applicant's race or color, or regarding applicant's complexion or color of skin, eyes, and hair.
Physical condition, handicap	Job-related physical examination or perform functions of the job with or without reasonable accommodation.	Questions regarding applicant's general medical condition, state of health, or receipt of Workers' Compensation or disabilities or handicaps.
Religion	Statement by employer of regular days, hours, or shifts to be worked.	Questions regarding applicant's religion, or religion preventing from weekend or holidays work.
Arrest,records	Have you ever been convicted of a felony or a misdemeanor and imprisoned?	Have you ever been stopped by a police officer while driving? Or arrested?

Subject	Acceptable	Unacceptable
Military service	Questions regarding relevant skills acquired from U.S. military service.	General questions regarding military service such as dates, discharge, reserve duty, and foreign military.
Activities	Job-related organizations, clubs, professional societies.	List all organizations, clubs, societies, and lodges to which you belong.
References	By whom were you referred for a position? Persons willing to provide professional and/or character references.	Questions that disclose race, color, names, creed, national origin, ancestry, physical handicap, medical condition, marital status, age, or sex.
ER notify	Name and address to notify person in an emergency is proper once hired.	Relationship or ethnicity of person to contact in an emergency.

Source: Department of Fair Employment Housing. 01/86.2000

or has filed for bankruptcy, he or she would undoubtedly be rejected. Consulting legal counsel can save costly time, emotions, and financial resources. Obtaining multiple opinions and using a search committee can also provide diverse viewpoints on employment selection.

The application for employment should always be reviewed and updated, if necessary, prior to beginning the search process to ensure current legal compliance. For example, statements that reveal an applicant's age, gender, ethnicity, religious creed, color, national origin, ancestry, or disability are generally unacceptable on the application.

In preparing for the interview, it is generally advisable to write out the questions in advance and ask each applicant the same questions. This information should also be documented and filed should there be an audit by a human rights agency or to defend a claim of discrimination. There are different state and federal guidelines regarding how long the records should be kept, which is generally two to three years.

If information is needed in order to complete a background check, questions about an applicant's assumed name may be necessary and permissible. However, asking a person's maiden name may reveal a person's ethnicity or race and is generally not acceptable, nor is it needed for making a decision whether or not an applicant can perform the essential functions of the job.

Also, asking questions about whether a name has been changed by a court order is generally unacceptable. For example, a parent may change the name of a child later in life, or a person may change his or her name due to a divorce or to have a more common name. However, it may be prudent if name changes were a result of felony convictions and the candidate is hiding past legal information.

During the interview session, asking questions to an applicant about his or her birthplace, parents, spouse, and other relatives are generally unacceptable, since it may reveal a person's national origin. Generally, in the United States an applicant does not need to be a U.S. citizen to be employed.

Rather, this person simply needs to be legally authorized to work in the country. It is necessary to obtain verification documents that a person is eligible to work in the country, but only after an offer of employment has been extended. Questions such as "Can you produce naturalization papers prior to employment?" or "Were you born in the United States?" are generally unacceptable.

An area that is less clear-cut involves hiring a bilingual or ESL teacher. The school board may desire to hire a teacher who has a strong cultural appreciation for Hispanic origin and may desire to hire a native fluent Spanish-speaking applicant from a Spanish country. The needs of the institution and best learning for the students should be considered.

It is generally unacceptable to have a requirement that the person be born in a Spanish country or his or her native language is Spanish. The essential question is "Can the applicant do the essential functions of the job," and the applicant's birthplace probably doesn't matter. Hiring the best qualified candidate for a job position is generally the best policy.

Questions regarding marital status and gender are generally inappropriate unless relevant to the job. If an organization is hiring a director of a Jewish women's organization, then it may be appropriate to seek a female who is Jewish. On the other hand, it is generally inappropriate to ask questions to an applicant about sex; marital status; number and ages of children or dependents; obligations for childcare, pregnancy, or childbearing or birth control that are irrelevant to performing the essential functions of the job.

Another area that has been somewhat controversial in school districts involves an applicant's race, gender, color, and ethnicity. Generally using these factors as a basis for hiring decisions are illegal but may be appropriate in special situations in meeting the affirmative action requirements, or when an organization has established a BFOQ.

An example of a BFOQ is a situation where a religious institution needs to hire a person of a specific religion to satisfy the job requirements. Also, in some cases a school district that has a student body that is 100 percent African American might seek an African American candidate for the principal of the school, or might need a woman to supervise a girls' locker room.

The school district may establish that race in this situation is an essential function to support the needs of the organization. Cases like this may involve potential for reverse discrimination. There have been many cases throughout the history of the United States where reverse discrimination has been charged. Given the myriad of affirmative action programs and evolving legislation, it is not always clear-cut, and legal counsel should be obtained.

Another controversial area in hiring involves the disability of an applicant. The *Americans with Disabilities Act* (ADA) *of 1990* prohibits employment discrimination against people with physical or mental disabilities who can perform the essential functions of the job with or without reasonable accommodations. Therefore, during an interview it is generally unacceptable to ask the applicant questions regarding his or her general medical condition, state of health, or other physical or mental disabilities.

It is also generally unacceptable to ask whether an applicant has filed past worker's compensation claims. Likewise, it is not advisable to discriminate against candidates for past health issues unless it poses a potential harm to students. These types of questions may reveal medical information that could be used to discriminate against the applicant.

A common question that can be asked by interviewers is "Can you perform the essential functions of the job you are applying for with or without reasonable accommodation?" This question gets to the heart of whether an applicant can perform the basic job, which should be the fundamental objective of the interview. Determining the definition of *reasonable accommodation* can be unclear.

Various legal experts have tried to define this term by using past case law. For example, it may be entirely appropriate and expected to spend a few hundred dollars to provide a ramp for wheelchair employee or special ergonomic support devices or cushions that can assist a disabled person in performing the essential functions a job. However, it may be an undue burden to require a school board to destroy an entire building and rebuild it with an expensive elevator to accommodate a disabled individual. Again, these are questions that school administrators need to consult with local legal counsel.

Another controversial area that has emerged in recent times is the religious affiliation and ability to work during school hours. It is acceptable to ask an applicant if he or she is able to perform the essential functions of the job and work hours. However, questions regarding the applicant's religion and observation of religious holy days are generally unacceptable.

This situation may pose controversy later if the employee's religious holy days fall on regular school days and the employee requests an extended leave of absence. Generally there are contractual personal leave days that can be used. However, this issue may be more problematic when an extended leave is desired.

Other questions regarding military service, organizational activities, and emergency notification need to be legally followed as well. Any questions that reveal a person's race, religious creed, color, national origin, ancestry, sex, or age that may be disclosed by answering these questions are generally unacceptable. However, asking an applicant to list all organizations or special military experiences that are relevant to the job is generally appropriate. Further information on these laws can be obtained from the EEOC.

Once the search committee has been well trained in preemployment laws, they need to prepare for conducting interview. Described here is a list of steps in conducting an interview session:

1. Interview preparation

   - Review questions (classified and nonclassified)
   - Review preemployment legal guidelines
   - Review and make copies of candidate's resume
   - Make copies of district benefits
   - Obtain copy of district materials (e.g., SIP, community, housing)
   - Make copy of organizational chart

2. Opening/icebreaker (make small talk, offer drink, obey legal guidelines)
3. Data check (confirm candidate and correct position)
4. School district overview (brief review of the school organization)
5. Candidate questions (use prepared standard questions)
6. Candidate needs

   - Record candidate's questions about the job
   - Ask what candidate desires in job or career

7. Promote the district (benefits, community, etc.)
8. Ask if a candidate has any questions
9. Close the session

   - Ask permission for reference check
   - Ask and obtain signature for background check
   - Ask permission and set up drug test
   - Explain next steps
   - Give tour of district or school

10. Post-session follow-up items

   - Debrief session with interviewing team
   - Make hiring decision
   - Document decisions and information
   - Check references

- Conduct background check
- Schedule drug test
- Complete employment form
- Prepare follow-up letter (next step or rejection letter)

During the interview preparation phase, the screening committee members should understand as much as they can about the school district. Applicants will undoubtedly have questions about the school district that will need to be answered. Some of these questions may relate to the union contract, human resource manual, benefits, community and business affiliation, housing availability, and so on. It is often good to prepare a copy of the organizational chart so that applicants can develop a clear understanding of the people and functions within the organization.

During the actual interview session it is important to start out with an icebreaker to make the applicant feel comfortable and to humanize the session. Questions about the traffic or weather are fairly innocuous and can be good icebreakers. The first formal questions are called *data check questions*, which are questions that confirm the applicant's name, the position being applied for, and start date. It is not unusual during an interview to find that the wrong applicant is applying for the wrong job at the wrong time, and starting out with a data check can help resolve these issues and prevent wasted time and further embarrassment to all parties.

Once the interview session begins, it is appropriate to start by introducing all the members of the committee, providing an overview of the school district. The interviewers then generally begin asking the applicant the formally prepared questions. Some typical interview questions include:

Describe your leadership style.

1. Describe your teaching style.
2. Describe your teaching philosophy.
3. List examples of professional skill development you have taken in the past five years?
4. Give us an example of how you have handled a difficult student disciplinary problem.
5. What are your greatest strengths?
6. What are your greatest weaknesses?
7. Describe your decision-making process in solving complex educational issues.

Many of the questions that are preprepared relate to categories such as instruction, curriculum, discipline, education, experience, interpersonal skills, and teaching style, and so on. Questions should be designed that allow the screening committee to obtain applicant information on how well the applicant can perform the essential functions of the job. During the interview session the members should pay close attention to the answers, document responses, and exhibit proper listening skills. Some examples include:

- Avoid overreacting to an applicant's statement.
- Avoid irritating distractions such as excessive writing that may distract the applicant.
- Maintain good eye contact.
- Demonstrate proper expressions and acknowledgment of applicant's statements.
- Avoid prejudging the applicant or establishing a positive or negative "halo" effect.
- Use effective nonverbal behaviors.
- Paraphrase the applicant's statements to gain assurance of understanding.
- Thank the applicant for his or her comments and questions.

A part of the interview session should allow the applicant to ask questions about the job and school district. Also it is often beneficial to provide a tour of the facilities and to promote the school district and community. This helps sell the school and establish good public relations even if the applicant does not take the job.

The closing of the interview session should not be abrupt and should conclude in a professional manner. Typical actions include asking for permission for reference checks, obtaining a signature for a background check, asking for permission to schedule a drug test or medical physical, and giving an explanation of the next steps in the process.

It is important during the closing that the members refrain from giving applicants an impression that they will receive a job offer. It is generally acceptable to inform the applicants that once all candidates have been interviewed and a decision has been made, they will be contacted.

After the interview session has concluded, much of the work begins with the postsession follow-up. This session is critical for the screening committee members to thoroughly evaluate the applicant and make decisions for the next steps. Table 2.2 provides a sample of a typical interview evaluation form.

There are many types of evaluation forms that can be used to assess an applicant after an interview. Every school district should develop a form that is best for the organization and is legally compliant. It is generally advisable to meet as soon as possible after an interview to capture everyone's impressions and review comments.

Table 2.2. Example of applicant evaluation

Name of Applicant: Interview Date:
Position: Lead Interviewer:
Please complete the questions below after interviewing the applicant.

	Unable to evaluate	Below average	Average	Above average	Excellent
Education (general background and knowledge)	0	1	2	3	4
Experience (practical teaching experience)	0	1	2	3	4
Interpersonal Skills (ability to relate to people)	0	1	2	3	4
Communication Skills (verbal, nonverbal, and written skills)	0	1	2	3	4
Technology Skills (proficiency in using technology)	0	1	2	3	4
				TOTAL SCORE _____	
Rating Recommendation (circle one)	Hire	Consider	Do not hire		

Comments

Interview Team:
1.
2.
3.

Some typical categories to evaluate include education knowledge, experience, interpersonal communication skills, and technology. The decision of whether to extend an offer to a candidate can also be made. Also comments justifying a member's rating decision should be documented. When completed, all interview evaluation forms should be collected, filed, and kept for future use should there be an audit or discrimination claim.

After completing reference checks and documenting all information, and once an offer has been extended to the candidate, then the background check and drug and medical exam often occur. The candidate is generally extended an offer for employment and signs a release form (permission to conduct

Table 2.3. Examples of applicant background checks

Search	Description
Social Security Verification	Verifies a valid social security number or use of multiple numbers or aliases.
Driver's License	Verifies driver's license, type, issue date, restrictions.
Credit History	Searches credit bureau reports on applicant's finances.
County Civil Record	Reviews all county civil litigation records available in the county court house.
County Criminal Record	Examines all criminal activity contained in the Clerk of Court's office as generally matched by name, date of birth, social security number, and address.
Federal Criminal Record	Examines U.S. federal district court house databases for records of federal crimes and violations.
Employment Verification	Seeks details on dates of employment, position, and job-related information of previous employment history.
Education Verification	Searches and verifies educational experience, institutions, date of attendance, and degrees obtained.
State Certifications and Licenses	Verifies Department of Education applicant's certification and licenses.
Sex Offender Registry Search	Examines all registered sex offenders and applicant's current and former residences.

the background check) prior to completion of medical exams or background checks. The school district also needs to obtain official transcripts and other certifications or licenses.

There are many types of investigations that can be conducted for the background check (see table 2.3). The investigation is performed by an outside agency and includes a search of public records on criminal convictions, incidents of dishonesty, moral turpitude, violence, drug-related offences, credit bureau information, history of driving infractions or accidents, previous employment records, and other possible public and proprietary records.

A written request is generally obtained within sixty days of any adverse action or decision, although these time periods may vary from school district to school district and investigative agency. Other typical information included in an investigation is the applicant's full legal name, addresses within the past five to ten years, previous names or aliases, social security number, date of birth, drivers' license number and state, and a complete signature and authorization date.

There are many guidelines when conducting *background checks* and employers must abide by federal and state laws to avoid harm to applicants and lawsuits. Investigations that have no apparent connection to the job should be avoided. Many states have *fair credit reporting acts* and standards for conducting employment background checks that need to be followed (Fair Credit Reporting Act, 2012).

For example, the State of California provides a summary of the State *Fair Credit Reporting Act* (FCRA) to all persons, which outlines their rights under the FCRA and what to do when their rights have been violated. According to the FCRA, when an outside agency prepares an investigative report, an applicant has a right to have notice if neighbors, friends, or associates have been interviewed regarding his or her character, general reputation, personal characteristics, or mode of living. Generally, there are statutes of limitations as well.

For example, negative information may not be reported after seven years. However, exceptions are often made for bankruptcy and other criminal convictions relevant to the job. Generally employers need to give an applicant a *preadverse action notice* with the background report if an adverse action has been taken.

In addition, federal law provides fair credit reporting act and publications that can assist both employers and applicants in following the fair credit standards and practices. Generally, all applicants have the right to know the extent of a background check and how it will be used for screening purposes. Applicants have rights, and permission must be obtained by the perspective employee.

Employers are subject to monetary penalties if applicants' rights are violated. However, some states may not require an employer to give an applicant a copy of the background check other than information obtained through public records. Examples of nonpublic record information include verification and information from past employers, information from individuals providing references, and third-party investigation data.

Some employers include a self-screening section that allows applicants to obtain a copy of public record information and to waive their rights for a copy of this information. If applicants do not waive their rights to receive a copy of public record information, they have approximately one week to obtain receipt. Also it is not uncommon that public records may contain inaccurate information about people. Generally an applicant can dispute in writing to the school district any inaccurate information obtained in the investigative public record report.

The applicant may need to obtain legal counsel to clarify discrepancies and correct the public record. Examples of inaccurate or outdated information may pertain to court records for criminal activity that have been expunged by the applicant. Each state also has different laws regarding information about arrests, indictments, and misdemeanor complaints. For example, the State of California allows any indictments and related matters that have not come to trial or have been resolved to be reported on a background check report.

There are also statutes of limitations on obtaining information on criminal convictions, arrests, and indictments. If a full pardon has been granted by law, then convictions cannot be on a report. There are many agencies that provide background check services with varying degrees of capabilities. Most agencies investigate public record databases, although there are more extensive private and federal databases. For example, the *Federal Bureau of Investigation* has a database called the *National Crime Information Center* (NCIC) that can in some cases be accessed in cooperation with the agency (National Crime Information Center, 2018). Generally, the FBI will need to know the type of job position and concern prior to cooperating or giving permission to use the database.

A school board must perform due diligence especially in verifying education, certification, and criminal and sex offender background checks to ensure the protection of students. Table 2.3 shows examples of a preemployment screening search items for an applicant's background check. This is a competitive business, and there are many different prices depending upon the extent of the screening services desired. Typical screening areas are social security verification, credit history reports, driver's license search, county criminal records search, federal criminal records search, employment verification, sex offender registry reports, and education and certification verification.

Another controversial issue that can arise during the screening process is the requirement of a *polygraph examination*. Organizations in general cannot require a job applicant to take an employment polygraph test. This requirement can only be done once the specific conditions are met, which involve a good-faith effort by the employer to ensure the safety and security of people within an organization.

This situation might include certain security or safety personnel of a school district that has a significant impact on the health and safety of the students and staff. Additional information on the use of polygraphs can be obtained through the *American Polygraph Association* and *State and Federal Department of Labor regulations*.

The use of *psychological* and *behavioral tests* and assessment centers has been controversial in the selection process. Generally these assessments have been reserved for administrative and specialized positions. For example, data processors may be required to demonstrate keyboarding proficiency, or security people may need to pass a safety procedures examination.

An administrator might be required to complete an *in-basket exercise* to demonstrate leadership and management decisions making proficiency. Sometimes assessment centers are used to screen candidates for a position through use of trained professionals. Discretion should be used when using assessment centers to ensure that there is adequate *construct validity* and a relationship between these assessment activities and the essential job functions.

Caution should also be given when using personality tests to assess an applicant. There are numerous personality tests that have evolved from the personality styles articulated by Carl Jung's four styles of the *thinker*, *doer*, *feeler*, and *intuitor* (Jung, 1923). However, human resources professionals must ensure that personality tests are not used to discriminate against people when making employment selections.

While assessing the personality style of an applicant may be interesting and somewhat useful in comparing existing team members' styles with an applicant, these tests should not be used as a sole reason for hiring a person. Also, the construct validity of these tests may be questionable given that people may demonstrate different styles depending upon the situation he or she is placed in. For example, while working under pleasant conditions, an employee may demonstrate one style, but under stressful conditions another style may be exhibited.

One of the difficult aspects in evaluating an applicant for a position involves making a determination whether there is a good fit between the applicant and the school. The search committee members should be aware of the myriad of applicant danger signs in hiring a person. Some of these are:

- Frequent and short employment.
- Employment history discrepancies.
- Actual job duty discrepancies.
- Applicant's refusal to consent to background check or references.
- False application or false submission of employment data.
- Extensive negative comments toward past employers.
- Unclear or confusing reasons for leaving past employers.

However, caution should be exercised when attempting to prejudge an applicant solely based upon these danger signs. For example, in the past, a frequent danger sign was the short duration of employment by a candidate. This is known as *job hopping* and might send a signal to prospective employer that an applicant may not be a long-term employee.

However, within the past couple decades the frequent changing of jobs has been more common among employees due to the economy. Therefore, less credence might be placed on applicants who change jobs frequently. Applicants who have gained a variety of experiences from different school districts may offer valuable knowledge and skills for a school district, especially at the administrative level.

Considerable legislative and legal attention has been given to federal and state laws concerning the recruiting, screening, interviewing, and hiring of applicants. Courts have tended to place the burden of proof on the school district rather than the applicant when determining whether discrimination has taken place. The school district needs to provide evidence that there has been no discrimination, disparate treatment, or adverse impact on applicants during this selection process. Federal law does provide protection for employers to allow legal discrimination when there is evidence of a BFOQ.

A BFOQ can be established when a school district demonstrates operational necessity for discriminating against a protected class or favors one person over another. For example, if an institution has a religious affiliation and requires that all employees be of a specific religious faith may constitute a BFOQ defense.

The BFOQ defense is generally more applicable to private schools than public schools. However, a public school might employ a BFOQ defense when the safety or health of students or employees is impacted. For example, a school district may impose a mandatory age requirement for bus drivers or in supervising students. If a lawsuit arises for a BFOQ, it can be costly and time-consuming for the school district. Past case law may help determine the legitimacy of a BFOQ, but ultimately the court will render the final decision.

The selection of the best candidate should be based upon the job description, needs of the organization, and legal compliance. The search committee members can use a spreadsheet listing the applicants' names in rank order and matched against the selection criteria. This information can be examined with the interview evaluation, applicant credentials, transcripts, references, and background check in making a selection decision.

The final decision to extend an offer of employment should be approved by the superintendent and/or school board. An important step in this process is to notify the applicants who have been selected for positions with a formal letter. The final offer for acceptance of employment is often contingent upon satisfactory completion of all background checks and medical examination. Also, special accommodations can be made, if necessary.

It is also common courtesy to send a letter to the applicants who have been rejected. Should the top selected candidate reject the offer, other candidates would then be considered. Also, when committee members talk to applicants who have been rejected, it is critical that this discussion be undertaken in a professional manner and they follow guidelines such as:

1. Be direct but personal.
2. Do not become defensive for the decision.
3. Do not make future promises or try to appease the applicant.
4. Be professional and courteous.
5. Document the discussion.
6. Do not become overly positive or give indications for future employment opportunities.
7. Do not disclose personal or investigation report information that should remain confidential.

The final completion of the interview and selection process concludes with documenting all information, filing the information, notifying all internal staff members, and making arrangements for the candidate's employment.

ORIENTING NEW EMPLOYEES

Once a candidate has been employed, the next step is to conduct a proper orientation and indoctrination program. This is especially important for new teachers and staff members entering the education institution for the first time. This program should provide an opportunity to clarify job responsibilities and expectations, understand the history of the school district, meet fellow teachers and staff members, understand policies and procedures, and become comfortable with the new work environment. Described here is a list of the typical employee orientation information covered for new employees:

1. District strategic plan
2. Vision and mission statements of the school
3. School improvement plan (SIP)
4. District policies and procedures, child abuse reporting, and so forth.
5. Solving difficulties, problems, and complaints
6. Hours of work
7. Performance reviews and evaluations
8. Infectious disease policies
9. Employee conduct and corrective action
10. Substance abuse policy and dress code
11. Benefits, staff development, holidays, and employee purchase and services
12. Compensation, pay procedures, and time records
13. Leave of absences: Personal , medical, and family leave
14. Work areas: Building evacuation and fire alarm, parking, safety, and security
15. Technology and software
16. Union contract and regulations

Many human resource manuals stipulate that organizations subscribe to an *employee at will* policy, which implies that employees are free to resign at any time without reason, and likewise, the organization has the right to terminate an employee's employment at any time with or without reason or notice. However, for employees who belong to a union, the contractual agreements would stipulate conditions for employment.

Also, while many private and charter schools may not have union contracts or employment agreements, federal and state laws would still apply. New employee processing often involves the employees obtaining necessary supplies and equipment to perform their work. Typical items often included are employee badges, key cards, photo identification badge, time-keeping information, technology equipment, computer user id and password, and work supplies.

New employees also have certain rights to human resource records and information as granted by federal and state laws (United States Equal Employment Opportunity Commission, 2011). For example, employees may have the right to review their file and to obtain a copy. Some information may be restricted such as letters of reference, and administrative planning information if the disclosure would constitute an unwarranted invasion of personal privacy. Also employees may have access to medical examination for conditions that do not pose a health or safety danger to others. Generally, new employees need to obtain a medical examination and be free from infectious diseases that can harm others. In addition, many organizations have nonsolicitation and distribution activities during work time and dress codes.

Other areas to be covered include parking arrangements, safety, security, computer software and supplies, use of copy machine, emergency evacuation procedures, and office management protocol in handling outside visitors. Other topics for new teachers include an overview of district teaching policies and procedures, blood-borne pathogens and infectious disease, curriculum and instruction expectations, and the teaching evaluation process.

A proper staff induction program is especially important for new teachers. Research has shown that up to one-third of new teachers leave a school district within three years (National Center for Education Statistics, 2018). There are several reasons for teacher attrition such as high expectations by administrators, long hours working on lesson plans, grading and handling student and parent issues. Therefore, providing meaningful new teacher orientation and mentoring programs can help support new teachers and reduce attrition.

New teacher induction generally begins with completing all the necessary federal and state employment forms. For example, the *I-9 Employment Eligibility Verification Form* is required by the *Department of Homeland Security* for all employees in the United States. The purpose of this form is to document all new employees whether they are a citizen of the United States or not.

This requirement became effective in November 1986 and requires information on citizenship and eligibility of people for employment in the United States. Employers are responsible for verifying employment authorization status and are required to obtain acceptable documents such as a U.S. passport, foreign passport, temporary immigrant visa, driver's license or identification card issued by a state within the United States that contains a photograph, voter's registration card, military card, social security card, or birth certificate.

There are some exceptions to these requirements such as non immigrant foreigners who are authorized to work in the country can show a foreign passport or other endorsements of the alien's nonimmigrant status. In cases where an employee is under the age of eighteen, documents that are permissible include a school record or report card, physician or hospital record, and day care or nursery record. In some cases a taxpayer identification number and certification may be required.

SUMMARY

The recruiting of applicants and orientation of employees is one that requires a systematic and comprehensive knowledge in recruiting, selecting, orientation, and indoctrination. The overall purpose is to select the best candidates for a position, provide the proper orientation and mentoring, and provide professional development that supports the employee's success within the organization. Moreover, incorporating an effective orientation program can help ensure that employees perform to the standards required by the organization and allow the school district to remain legally compliant.

There are numerous resources available to assist educators in this entire process and should be utilized to develop the best systems and processes that are relevant for an organization. Moreover, developing a collaborative approach with involvement by all stakeholders can help to ensure agreement and success to the recruiting and professional development programs.

CASE STUDY

You have been recently hired as the school principal for Edwards High School in southeastern United States. The school has approximately 1,200 students and a teaching faculty who are mainly white, middle-aged men. The academic performance of the students is average as compared to other school districts in the state. There has not been much involvement of the parents or community within the school. Due to budgetary constraints class size has been high with most classes containing thirty-five to forty students.

Also, there is a need for replacing several teachers who will be retiring at the end of the school year as well as several classified staff. Some of the facilities are old and need to be replaced, such as student wheelchair ramps, broken windows, and collapsed fences along the school grounds.

The superintendent has also mentioned to you that the performance evaluation system is outdated and that some local area school districts have been using a new computerized appraisal system. He also mentioned that Edward High School has never had a mentoring program, since they have not needed to hire new employees for several years. Overall, the school board and superintendent have high hopes for you as a new principal.

The school board and superintendent have charged you, as the new principal, to submit six goals for the high school for the ensuing school year. Based upon the information in this case, please develop six goals and list them in priority order.

Exercises and Discussion Questions

1. List the steps and characteristics for developing a comprehensive recruiting program at a school.
2. List and describe some of the relevant federal, state, and school laws and policies impacting selection process.
3. List the characteristics of an effective new teacher orientation program.
4. Outline the types of topics for a typical new employee orientation program.
5. List the five categories and examples for a professional development program.
6. Describe some major reasons for establishing a new employee orientation program.
7. Describe some of the typical problems in interviewing applicants for a position.
8. List and describe some of the pertinent federal and state EEOC laws when orientating a new employee to the job.
9. Describe how to keep all employees informed about who are new employees in a school district.
10. List and describe several questions when interviewing an applicant for a teacher position.

REFERENCES

Fair Credit Reporting Act. State of California. (2012).

Jung, C. (1923). *Psychological Types*. New York: Harmony Books.

National Center for Education Statistics. (2018). https://nces.ed.gov/pubsearch/pubsinfo.asp?pubid=2009062.

National Crime Information Center. (2018). www.ncic.org/2018.

United States Equal Employment Opportunity Commission. (2011). www.eeoc.gov.

Chapter 3

Mentoring, Professional Development, and Performance Evaluations

Objectives

At the conclusion of this chapter you will be able to:

1. Understand new employee mentoring procedures used by school and corporate leaders (ELCC 3.1, PSEL 3).
2. Differentiate between federal and state laws that impact employee evaluation practices (ELCC 6.1, 6.2, 6.3, PSEL 6).
3. Understand methods of professional development (ELCC 3.1, PSEL 3).
4. Describe different types of performance appraisal forms (ELCC 3.1, 3.3, PSEL 3).
5. Understand different strategies in conducting performance evaluations (ELCC 2.1, 3.3, PSEL 3).
6. Describe the process of appraising employees' performance (ELCC 3.3, 6.1, PSEL 3, 6).

MENTORING EMPLOYEES

One of the most effective strategies that can support a new employee is a mentoring program. Assigning an experienced employee who can act as a mentor for the new employee on matters such as dealing with conflicts, policies, personal issues, and administrative requirements can help contribute to successful employment. The mentor can also help orientate the new employee to the organization and provide effective coaching on the new employee's performance.

Dedicated, committed, credible, and experienced are generally prerequisites for teacher mentors. In addition, all mentors should be well trained in how to be an effective coach. Topics might include understanding instruction and curriculum, managing student discipline, and understanding the school district operations and district policies and procedures. In addition to these professional qualities, an effective mentor needs effective coaching qualities, which include being sensitive, a good listener, empathetic, accessible, supportive, honest, and trustworthy.

For example, while there may be added costs to the school district for these programs, the time and money that can be saved by not needing to conduct a search to replace teachers can well justify the program. Some benefits for the teacher mentor include additional compensation, release time, satisfaction of helping others, and support for the school district.

The components of a good mentoring program consist of establishing rapport with the new teacher, establishing mutual expectations, providing ample resources, observing the teacher, and providing meaningful feedback (see figure 3.1). Also, a good mentoring program should be designed to allow for regular observations of the new teacher, time for providing coaching, and time for following up on performance issues.

Mentors should also, in turn, be evaluated by administrators to ensure that their performance is acceptable. Figure 3.2 lists and describes the typical information for a teacher mentoring program. A good mentoring program includes these items as well as the resources needed to implement the mentoring. Top administration support and active teacher participation are also keys to a successful program.

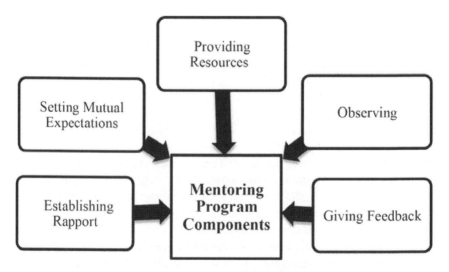

Figure 3.1. Components of an effective mentoring program.

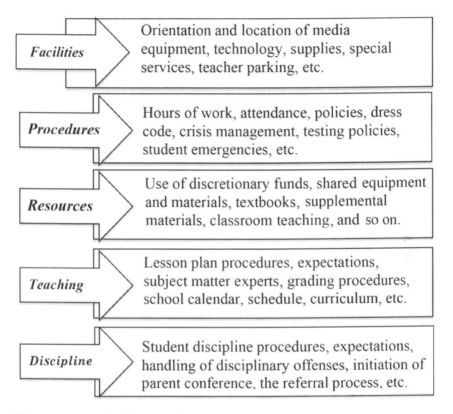

Facilities — Orientation and location of media equipment, technology, supplies, special services, teacher parking, etc.

Procedures — Hours of work, attendance, policies, dress code, crisis management, testing policies, student emergencies, etc.

Resources — Use of discretionary funds, shared equipment and materials, textbooks, supplemental materials, classroom teaching, and so on.

Teaching — Lesson plan procedures, expectations, subject matter experts, grading procedures, school calendar, schedule, curriculum, etc.

Discipline — Student discipline procedures, expectations, handling of disciplinary offenses, initiation of parent conference, the referral process, etc.

Figure 3.2. **Examples of content of a mentor program.**

When working with a new teacher, the mentor should begin by establishing rapport. He or she should cover the basic teaching responsibilities, lesson plan preparation, strategies in beginning a class, completing student absentee records, and classroom management. Other items might include dealing with student academic problems, responding to a fire or disaster drill, writing a syllabus and course outline, and dealing with parent issues.

One of the most important topics to cover with a new teacher is time management. The new teacher needs to become proficient in multitasking skills. Some of the common time wasters for a new teacher include telephone interruptions, inadequate planning, oversocializing, meetings, procrastinating, dealing with confused responsibilities or expectations, poor communications, and personal disorganization.

A good mentor should coach the new employee on these time wasters and offer strategies for overcoming them which might include listing goals for each day, preparing work in advance, making a daily to-do list, eliminating unproductive activities, and setting deadlines for accomplishing work tasks. The mentor needs to understand the emotional and professional needs of the new teacher and strive to maintain confidence and trust with the teacher.

For example, the mentor should make regular observations of the new teacher's instruction and provide feedback. The basic steps for conducting a teacher observation include preconference, observation, analysis, and postconference feedback. During the preconference discussion, the mentor schedules the time and place for observation in collaboration with the new teacher. During the observation, the mentor should record and evaluate the new teacher on all aspects of teaching and classroom management.

Afterward, a careful analysis and review of the information should be completed in preparation for the postconference meeting. During this meeting the mentor should give constructive feedback to the new teacher. At times the mentor may need to provide on-the-job training for the new teacher, which includes five basic steps as outlined in table 3.1.

The mentor should regularly provide casual feedback by asking questions such as "Describe things that are going well for you," "Describe some areas that you would like to improve," "What can I do as a mentor to better assist you?" The feedback given to new teachers by the mentor should be done on a formative versus summative basis. Formative feedback is an ongoing review designed to give informal assessment without the formal supervisory evaluation that becomes part of the new teacher's performance record.

This process allows the new teacher to freely ask questions and to improve performance without the worry of the feedback being used against him or her. Summative feedback is conducted generally by the new employee's supervisor and is used as a formal and official record of performance. Described here is a list of steps in conducting a formative coaching session.

1. Describe the performance.
2. State expectations or standards.

Table 3.1. The five steps to on-the-job mentor training

Steps (5 Ps)	Description
Plan	Make preparations for the on-the-job demonstration.
Present	Demonstrate the behavior (instruction or handling of a discipline problem).
Create a **P**ositive environment	Establish a good rapport and give good, positive atmosphere for teacher.
Perform the behavior	The new teacher performs the behavior while the mentor observes.
Performance evaluation	The mentor gives immediate feedback and follows up with teacher.

3. Ask new teacher for reflection.
4. Listen, empathize, and paraphrase.
5. Collaboratively identify the root cause.
6. Ask for suggestions on actions to improve.
7. Discuss and agree upon actions.
8. Thank the new teacher and build confidence.

During the first step of the formative coaching session the mentor should *describe the performance* of the new teacher. During this stage the mentor begins by humanizing the setting, and being objective but direct in describing performance that needs to be improved. For example, issues might include improving instruction, handling a student disciplinary case, or improving lesson plans.

Step two requires the mentor to describe the *desired expectation* or standard. For example, the mentor may state that lesson plans need to be error-free, well organized, and contain all components outlined in the school policy manual. This is a critical step and ensures that there is a mutual understanding of expectations.

Step three involves the new teacher *reflecting upon his or her performance* and identifying positive behaviors and areas in need of improvement. This reflection can be a valuable method to help a new teacher examine his or her performance without the mentor directly stating the problem. For example, the new teacher may conclude that he or she is having difficulty handling student misbehavior and needs to more thoroughly understand and administer the school district student disciplinary policies.

An important step in the formative coaching session is for the mentor to *sincerely listen*, empathize with his or her feelings, and paraphrase the new teacher's comments (step four). The use of paraphrasing helps to verify what the new teacher stated and confirm mutual understanding. This technique is popular among counselors and teachers to ensure there is active listening and helps develop trust among the people.

Typical statements might be "I can understand how you feel in a situation like this," "I can see how someone would have these feelings in a situation like this," or "I was once a new teacher as well and understand." Paraphrasing can also help to show that the mentor is demonstrating active listening and helps in personalizing the conversation and developing an atmosphere of respect.

Step five involves the new teacher identifying the *root cause* of the performance problem. This step is similar to step three but goes into greater detail. For example, if a new teacher is experiencing difficulty in handling disciplinary problems, the potential root causes might include distractions from outside influences, health issues, a poor attitude, need for additional training, or a dysfunctional school environment. It is important for the mentor to reinforce the new teacher's responsibility for improvement and to provide encouragement for improvement.

The sixth step entails asking the new teacher for solutions for the performance issue. In this way the new teacher is more likely to accept the solution. It also allows the new teacher to take responsibility for his or her own behavior. For example, the new teacher may need to include more engaging instructional activities or learn to control his or her emotions when dealing with misbehavior.

In step seven, the mentor and new teacher should discuss and agree upon an action plan for resolving the performance issue. There may be some negotiation, so they can collaboratively resolve the issue. The new teacher should propose a solution that is acceptable to the mentor, since he or she will be more apt to accept the solution rather than it being imposed upon him or her.

However, if the new teacher's suggestion is unacceptable to the mentor, further discussion may be necessary, and ultimately they will need to mutually arrive to an effective action. The last step, step eight, involves the mentor *thanking the new teacher* for participating in the coaching session and building his or her confidence. Building the confidence of a new teacher has reinforcing consequences.

Even if a mentor has difficulty in supporting a new teacher, especially for very poor performance incidents, the mentor needs to continue to maintain a positive working relationship; otherwise the mentor–new teacher relationship will be undermined. During the coaching process the mentor should also be aware of his or her subtle, nonverbal cues that the new teacher may observe that are incongruent with the mentor's verbal message. The mentor may also suggest a follow-up session to review the new teacher's progress and/or additional measures.

When giving constructive feedback, a mentor needs to be aware of the typical *defense mechanisms* that are often displayed by new teachers (see figure 3.3). Defense mechanisms are those things that human beings do to protect themselves from experiencing bad feelings. New teachers can often feel vulnerable, especially if they experience several setbacks.

Consequently, they may resort to defense mechanisms to prevent themselves from feeling bad. Understanding defense mechanisms can help a mentor in coaching the new teacher. New teachers may not resort to all of these defense mechanisms, but if the mentor sees patterns of one occurring he or she can be in a better position to coach the new teacher.

PROFESSIONAL DEVELOPMENT

Every employee, regardless if he or she is a new teacher, should be involved in professional development. Professional development is an ongoing process

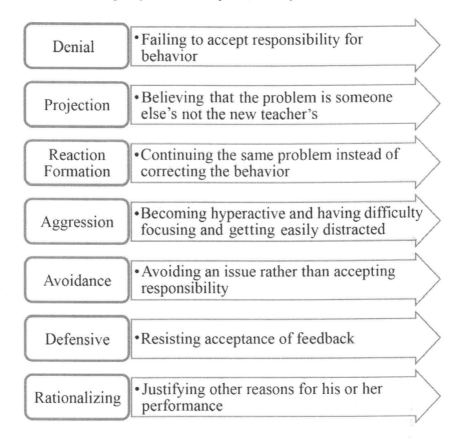

Figure 3.3. Typical defense mechanisms when mentoring.

and should be mutually designed by district administrators, department chairpersons, and teachers. Figure 3.4 outlines five common categories of professional development.

For example, the selection of topics should be completed through collaboration with teacher and administrators in order to achieve mutual ownership. Involvement in professional learning communities can be a good topic for professional development for new teachers. There are five categories of professional development that can offer a viable approach to achieving quality programs.

While new teachers are often academically prepared for teaching, they sometimes lack the essential skills of self-management. The ability to effectively meet administrative demands, handle school problems, solve day-to-day problems, and inspire students requires highly developed self-management skills. This requires both academic and emotional intelligence skills.

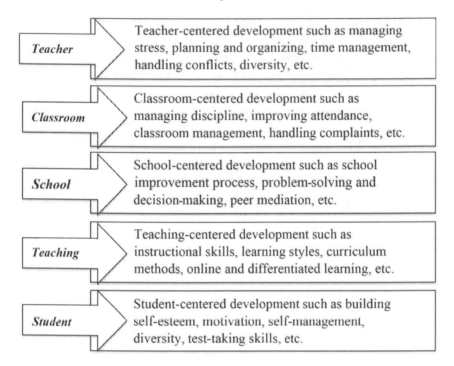

Figure 3.4. Categories of professional development.

Some of these skills include managing strong emotions, planning and organizing, handling conflict, understanding personal value and human relations, interpersonal communications, leadership, and motivation. These topics can provide meaningful personal growth for new teachers, as well as experienced teachers, and help them become more effective in the classroom.

Classroom-Centered Development

Student discipline continues to be a major problem in our schools today. Learning new strategies to effectively handle student misbehavior is especially critical for new teachers. Other topics include managing the classroom, teaching challenging students, motivating students, improving attendance, managing conflict, handling complaints, counseling students, understanding legal issues involved in disciplining students, and creating classroom strategies. Developing skills in managing the classroom environment will directly contribute to students' achievement and quality of school life.

School-Centered Development

School-centered topics focus on developing new teacher skills that contribute directly to meeting school organizational needs. These areas include developing skills in parent–community relations; managing change; developing a school improvement plan; managing and coordinating educational resources, finances, and teamwork; improving the school culture, and understanding professional learning communities. The educational leadership should include the entire staff in selecting the school-centered skills, so everyone can create a collaborative approach in meeting school needs.

Teaching-Centered Development

Teaching-centered development is a fundamental requirement of all new and experienced teachers if they are to continue to make a difference in student learning. Some skill development areas include action research, instructional methodology, curriculum development, learning styles, multiple intelligences, multiculturalism, and strategies for student achievement. The field of education is rapidly changing, and the need to keep abreast of current instructional and curricular programs and technology is critical for all teachers.

Student-Centered Development

The last category focuses on student-centered activities that can directly help student performance and personal management. Topics include building self-esteem, understanding individual differences, values and human relations, personal motivation and success, test-taking, interpersonal relationships, study habits, handling stress, dealing with gangs and peer pressure, and making life choices. Helping teachers to learn to more effectively improve the skills students use to deal with individual problems can significantly contribute to developing their academic and personal growth.

School administrators can use a number of techniques to develop a *professional development program* such as faculty surveys, staff focus groups, needs assessments, teacher interviews, and staff development committees. These methods can be beneficial in identifying the professional development needs of teachers and staff.

Administrators also need to understand that professional development is an ongoing process and should not expect instant miracles. The success of any professional development program is dependent upon the top administrators' support. School administrators should also celebrate achievements and recognize good performance of teachers who utilize the principles and strategies learned through these developmental programs.

Administrators can employ methods of professional development other than traditional workshops and seminars. Examples of other methods include using the performance evaluation session as a way to improve teachers' performance, undertaking research and development projects, including new teachers in committees, conducting staff meetings, conducting field trips to other schools, participating in professional associations, trying out team teaching, and providing professional development sessions during teacher in-service days.

PERFORMANCE EVALUATION AND LEARNING FRAMEWORKS

An effective performance evaluation system needs to be a component of a *Professional Learning and Growth framework.* For example, figure 3.5 illustrates a framework for achieving a vision of increasing student performance. There are typically three components of a framework: the teacher evaluation model, supervision, and evaluation. The teacher evaluation component should include one of the research-based models or a custom-developed model by the school district.

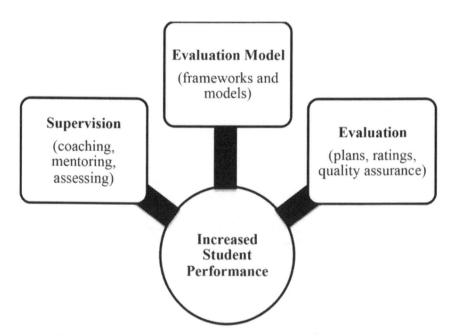

Figure 3.5. Professional learning and growth framework.

The supervision and evaluation components of a framework might include evaluating, coaching, mentoring, remediating, performance ratings, and quality assurance. This framework can also be useful as a visual method for all stakeholders to understand the components of a professional learning and growth framework.

Virtually every school district conducts performance evaluations. For example, the State Department of Education, local school district policies, union contractual agreements, and federal programs such as *Every Student Succeeds Act* are some of the proponents of performance evaluations. There has been an increased emphasis on accountability and standards and, in turn, performance evaluations have increased. Using the performance evaluation process can be an important tool in helping improve the performance of all teachers and staff within the school district.

Significant changes are being implemented that place greater emphasis on using multiple measures of assessment and professional learning and growth of teachers. Most of the states require objective measures of student performance such as classroom observations of teacher performance and actual student growth. Likewise, states are requiring that teachers receive professional development and coaching to help improve identified deficiencies.

The *National Council on Teacher Quality* conducted an extensive study of teacher evaluations and effectiveness and identified several policies that states are requiring in the teacher evaluation program. The trend is that states are including increased requirements for teacher accountability, professional learning and growth, student performance, and collaborative evaluations (Tomal et al., 2015).

Most states require multiple annual observations of teacher performance, provisions for probationary teacher, and specified performance improvement measures. For example, many states also specify the number of annual observations, timing of the observations, postobservations, and whether the observations are announced or unannounced. Professional learning and growth and teacher training are requirements in most state evaluation programs.

Several states also require that teacher evaluators complete and pass teacher evaluation courses to evaluate and provide identified professional learning counseling for teachers. For example, it is typical that teachers who have deficiencies in performance partake in a teacher improvement plan supervised under a qualified teacher evaluator.

Other policies that are being included in teacher evaluation programs include compensation-based performance, layoff provisions, licensure advancement, and licensure reciprocity teacher effectiveness considerations. The *National Council on Teacher Quality* states that all teachers should receive a minimum of an annual performance evaluation. The evaluation should use multiple evaluators or classroom observers when possible and provide teacher evaluator training for high-quality teacher evaluation programs and differentiate according to teacher need.

For example, in the State of Illinois, all teacher evaluators must complete and pass the teacher evaluator training program, as provided by the *Performance Evaluation Reform Act of 2010* and Senate Bill 7 and articles 24A and 34 of the Illinois School Code. Other states, such as Indiana and New York, require that teacher evaluators be effective teachers for the certification process.

Evaluation measures and observation rubrics are becoming mandatory in many states. For example, some states such as Connecticut, Indiana, Delaware, and Georgia are requiring *student learning objectives* (SLOs) as a component in the teacher evaluations to help assess teacher effectiveness and student performance goals. Georgia includes the SLOs as a critical component of the process called the *Teacher Key Effective System.*

Another performance assessment being used by some states is the use of peer, student, and parent surveys. The use of these assessments can provide additional measures of teacher effectiveness by gaining input from the people that educators serve. However, caution must be exercised to ensure that the assessment instruments are valid and reliable. School districts may want to consult experts to help write, administer, and interpret the surveys.

The role of unions in the evolution of teacher evaluations has been significant. There have been several differences in positions of unions and school boards regarding the use of multiple measures of teacher evaluations and connection to teachers' employment and compensation. The combination of strained financial resources and expanded teacher evaluations has exasperated the situation among state education agencies, school boards, and teacher unions.

For example, financial constraints and ideology differences in teacher evaluations have been creating tensions between school boards and teacher unions as demonstrated by the September 2012 Chicago teachers' strike. There were many issues involved such as pay, benefits, class size, school closing procedures, and teacher evaluation. This has had a major impact on the community and students in this third-largest school district in the nation.

Besides, Chicago, other states and cities across the nation are facing pressures for school change. Colorado and New Jersey public schools have implemented new statewide teacher evaluation program. Also, California and New York public schools have initiated program reductions and teacher evaluations. Likewise, substantial changes to teacher recruitment and teacher effectiveness have occurred in Kentucky.

Ultimately, teacher unions, school boards, and state departments of education need to work together in establishing and making changes to teacher evaluations, professional development, and hiring and terminating teachers.

The pressures of fiscal constraints and lack of other resources are pressuring the need for improvements in the teacher evaluation process. Collaboration and effective communications among all parties can help to resolve disputes and create workable and meaningful teacher evaluation and professional learning programs.

GOAL SETTING AND TEACHER EVALUATIONS

The goal-setting process and teacher evaluation are often integrally linked to the *school improvement plan* (SIP) and the teacher professional growth needs. Essentially, the process involves setting goals, as part of the SIP, and then evaluating teachers' performance regarding how well they accomplished the goals. This process often involves steps such as developing *values*, *mission*, *vision*, *major goals*, *key strategies*, and *key performance indicators*.

A school *vision* can be viewed as a public declaration that includes thoughtful reflection regarding the desired picture of the organization, or *what you seek to become*. For example, a vision statement might consist of becoming a happy, caring, tolerant, and collaborative environment where students are free to be creative and expressive in achieving successful learning. The vision sets the intended outcome of the school and is more concrete than a mission statement and is often based on the values and culture of the school.

Once the vision is established, the *major goals* are developed. These major goals are often written using SMART criteria—*specific*, *measurable*, *attainable*, *realistic*, and *timely*. The major goals are often directed to areas such as student performance, graduation rates, discipline, and attendance.

Once the major goals are written, *key strategies* must be developed. "A goal cannot be done." For example, if someone wants to become a millionaire, the *key strategy* outlines the process in "how to get the money." If a major school goal is to improve student standardized performance, then actions need to be established to accomplish the goal.

Included within the key strategy should be well-written *key performance indicators* (KPIs) or *metrics*. These KPIs are the score cards upon which the level of performance is to be established. For example, if the major goal is to improve students' technological knowledge of software application, then the key strategy might be providing online training for the students with a key performance indicator of achieving 50 percent competency within three months.

The entire process then concludes with an evaluation of the teachers and others in how well they accomplished the major goals. Teacher evaluation programs that include a goal-setting component might also be called *performance-based goals* or SLOs. These performance-based goals are based on student progress and are generally aligned with curriculum and instruction standards.

Many school districts also connect the performance goals to a district teaching framework. For example, the goals could be written to support the domains of the teaching framework: planning and preparation, classroom environment, instruction, and professional responsibilities (Danielson, 2007). The State of Ohio has adopted a goal-setting process that incorporates a self-assessment and analysis of student data (Ohio Teacher Evaluation System, 2018).

There are many reasons for conducting performance evaluations. Described here is a list of common reasons.

1. Provide performance feedback
2. Help motivate people
3. Promote communications
4. Use as a basis for staff development
5. Validate and document performance
6. Document performance problems
7. Comply with legal mandates
8. Provide rewards for people
9. Maintain fairness and accountability

The performance evaluation should not be a single-purpose process whereby the supervisor quickly completes a form, holds a brief appraisal session, files the form, and then goes back to business as usual. The supervisor should not consider the performance evaluation as busy work or as a *compliance exercise* just to satisfy school district or legal requirements.

This feeling by supervisors may exist when evaluating tenured faculty. Some supervisors may feel handicapped in evaluating low-performing, tenured teachers when union contractual obstacles make it difficult to terminate a tenured teacher. Supervisors should not take the easy way out and complete a quick or shallow performance review.

Performance evaluations can be a mechanism for accomplishing many goals. One reason for the evaluation is to give genuine constructive performance feedback to the employee, which can reinforce good performance and identify areas in need of improvement. The review session can also provide an opportunity to motivate employees through intrinsic verbal praise and a basis for extrinsic rewards such as salary increases and bonuses.

The performance evaluation session can serve to help promote communications, review respective performance, and develop continuous improvement plans for the future. This communication can serve as a basis for further developing people by establishing goals and gaining input that can help the entire organization.

Another reason for conducting the performance evaluation session is to validate and document the performance of employees. This documentation serves as a record for employee performance, which is needed when there is a need to terminate the employee in the future. Complying with legal and district policies is another reason to document performance problems. Lastly, the performance evaluation session can help to support personal accountability and provide a basis for the financial rewarding of employees.

While many people experience some anxiety during the performance review session, the benefits generally outweigh the time and effort. The performance evaluation session can provide an opportunity for documenting the employee's performance and serve as a system of fairness by informing employees how well they are performing in the organization.

There are many types of performance evaluation systems such as narrative appraisals, formative and summative assessments, 360 rating systems, and goal-based evaluations. Some organizations utilize an *open narrative evaluation*, especially for high-level administrators and managers. In this system the subordinate is asked to write a narrative regarding how well he or she performed during the year. This narrative is then used as a basis for performance review session. This type of system is a more informal approach and is infrequently used.

The *formative assessment* is often used to support the summative evaluation process. During the formative assessment, informal feedback is given to the employee by the supervisor, and this information is not used as part of the employee's permanent evaluation record. The whole idea of formative assessment is to give informal feedback without the fear of the information negatively impacting the employee's performance. However, it is sometimes difficult to entirely disregard the information when preparing a summative report.

The *summative evaluation* is the most popular approach and consists of a combination of rating assessment and narrative section on the evaluation form. The evaluation forms can consist of a paper copy and filed in a cabinet or an electronic copy and stored in a computer. The *360 performance evaluation* is a system that uses a multi-rater feedback process to obtain an evaluation on an employee. The feedback is generally provided by multiple supervisors, peers, support staff, community members, and possibly students.

This system began during the 1950s in the corporate world and gradually gained popularity among human resources professionals. However, the system has been somewhat controversial in that it requires extensive time to collect the feedback, and some people feel that the information is not always accurate or used exclusively for developmental purposes.

The 360 feedback may require gaining information from up to six to ten people. Each one of these individuals needs to complete an assessment of the employee. Sometimes the employee is allowed to choose the raters in addition to the supervisor. There are many decisions to be made in using a 360 approach such as the selection of the type of feedback instrument, number of raters, how the raters are selected, the process to be used, degree of confidentiality, anonymity of the raters, and how to integrate the information into the performance management system.

One advantage of the 360 process is that the employee receives multiple assessments. This may be more valuable than simply obtaining feedback from one supervisor. Also, when feedback is received from multiple stakeholders, a more diverse and comprehensive assessment can be obtained. However, this process takes more time than traditional performance evaluation processes and needs the cooperation and commitment of the reviewers.

The traditional *combination rating* and *open-comment evaluation* are still probably the most popular rating forms. The evaluation of an employee is generally conducted on a semi-annual or annual basis. Nontenured teachers are generally evaluated on a semi-annual basis and tenured teachers evaluated annually. Every organization needs to adopt the best schedule for the institution and state requirements.

Conducting evaluations on a semi-annual basis provides a good opportunity to obtain regular feedback, although this can be time-consuming for both the employee and supervisor. Typically, the annual review is the requirement by school districts and State Department of Education. Also the use of computer software has greatly increased the efficiency in completing and storing the evaluation forms into one database.

Regardless of the performance evaluation system used, there can be many problems associated with conducting the evaluation session, as outlined here:

1. Poor preparation and hasty review
2. Leniency effect
3. Central tendency rating
4. Recency effect rating
5. Poor inter-rater reliability
6. Personal prejudice and bias
7. Game playing
8. Rater indecisiveness
9. Being overly judgmental or emotional
10. Being overly confrontational and directive
11. Conducting a shallow review

One problem is having sufficient time to prepare the form and complete the review session. The *leniency effect* occurs when a supervisor rates an employee too high in all the performance factors. This may happen when the supervisor desires to avoid dealing with potential employee dissatisfaction or resistance. The supervisor may also overrate an employee to avoid creating conflict with the employee. *Central tendency* occurs when the supervisor rates all the performance factors in the middle of the scale.

One of the most difficult aspects in completing performance evaluation is to ensure that all supervisors strive to have a common understanding of what constitutes the performance standards of an employee, a term called *inter-rater reliability*. It is generally advisable that all supervisors participate in performance evaluation training to understand the criteria for rating employees and different levels of *standards of performance.*

Another problem with rating employees involves the human effect of harboring prejudice or bias toward an employee that may influence the rating. While the performance evaluation should be conducted objectively, it is nearly impossible to exclude personal subjectivity. *Game playing* is another problem with performance evaluations, which occurs when a supervisor over- or underrates an employee to support organizational politics.

For example, if a new teacher is being rated during the first six months, the supervisor may rate the teacher lower to help protect himself or herself later should the supervisor desire to terminate the teacher for cause or deny the teacher tenure. The supervisor may also rate an employee lower in order to allow the employee *room to grow*. All these examples are *game playing* and should be avoided.

The supervisor should also avoid being too judgmental, emotional, directive, or controlling during the performance evaluation session. Other problems associated with conducting a performance evaluation include:

- Rating an employee based upon personal characteristics that violate discrimination laws.
- Telling the employee about the rating or performance of other employees in the organization.
- Changing a rating during the employee session because of undue pressure by the employee.
- Conducting the session in a nonprivate location.
- Focusing the appraisal review session on the supervisor's performance rather than largely on the employee.
- Giving false promises to an employee to avoid conflict with the employee.
- Rating the employee exceptionally high in an effort to gain the employee's favor and support.
- Rating the employee low with the ulterior purpose of withholding a pay raise.
- Overweighting of recent occurrences that are either favorable or unfavorable and omitting past performance.

Most performance evaluation forms contain *performance rating levels* and *definitions*. For example, it is common to have a *five-level rating system* ranging from unacceptable to exceptional. Some forms have a three-level rating system consisting of not satisfactory, satisfactory, and outstanding. The following information provides the typical five-level performance rating with definitions.

Exceptional

Employee's performance excels in all aspects of the job, having reached the ultimate in job performance on a sustained basis. Performance is a quality found only in a small percentage of people within the organization. Performance is recognizable as being consistently distinguished, which far exceeds all expectations of required job standards. Employee demonstrates a very high degree of expertise and serves as a model of excellence to other employees. This level of performance compares with the best the school has seen. Quality of work is superior.

Exceeds Expectations

Employee's performance clearly and consistently is beyond the criteria and standards required of a fully competent person at all times. Performance is beyond the level expected in fulfilling job requirements and achieving goals and objectives without any supervision. Employee demonstrates proficiency in performing the difficult and complex aspects of the job competently and thoroughly, including extra or unique tasks assigned and often surpasses expectations. Quality of work is very good.

Meets Expectations

Employee's performance meets the criteria and standards of job performance for all aspects of the job. Performance is steady, reliable, and is maintained with a minimum of supervision. Employee consistently demonstrates the expected standard of performance, which means accomplishing his or her goals and objectives as well as generally meeting all required job standards. Quality of work is good.

Needs Improvement

Employee's performance usually meets the normal requirements in most of the job areas but occasionally fails to meet minimum criteria and standards of job performance. This rating would also apply to employees new to a position who are still learning all the aspects of the position. Performance at this level requires some improvement in order to meet or exceed the expectations of the job. Quality of work is inconsistent. This employee requires more than the normal guidance and direction.

Unacceptable

Employee's performance falls substantially short of the criteria and standard of job performance. Performance frequently fails to meet minimum requirements and objectives of almost all aspects of work. Employee demonstrates work clearly below the level of acceptability, and immediate and substantial improvement is necessary. Quality of work is poor. Significant improvement is needed.

The rating levels should be explained to supervisors and employees, so they have a common understanding of the *standards of performance*. There should be common agreement among supervisors regarding the general measures of performance. Supervisors should meet to review the overall percentages of the past ratings for each of the performance levels. For example, supervisors may feel that there are about 10 percent of employees who perform at the *exceptional* level, 45 percent who *exceed expectations*, 40 percent who *meet expectations*, 3 percent who *need improvement*, and only about 2 percent who are *unacceptable*.

While these percentages should not be required, the establishment of the percentages can help provide some general guidance and expectations for supervisor ratings. Establishing these general rating guidelines can also discourage *rating inflation* by supervisors.

The general performance factors contained in performance appraisal forms can vary dependent upon the type of position such as exempt/classified employees (e.g., teachers, administrators, managers, assistant superintendents, superintendent) or nonexempt/nonclassified employees (e.g., custodians, support staff, administrative assistants, safety and security employees).

Some performance evaluation forms contain more than one section of factors to be rated. For example, the first section might contain *job performance factors*, which are linked directly to the employee's job description. These forms tend to be performance-based and highly value the job description of the employees. They tend to be more rigid in the factors and less flexibility in subjective ratings.

If there are too many responsibilities in the job description, they are often combined so that the total number of factors is about five or six. These factors are then rated using a standard scale directly related to specific job responsibilities of the employee. The second section of the evaluation form often includes the *general performance factors*. Examples include quality and quantity of work, communication and interpersonal skills, dependability and reliability, ethics and service, collaboration, and safe work procedures.

Some evaluation forms may have a third section containing *performance goals*. This section is often reserved for upper-level administrators. The premise of including a *performance goals section* is to support the achievement of the school improvement plan initiatives and goals of the school district. In this case, administrators would write performance goals for the ensuing year that are approved by the board of education or supervisor.

The idea of writing goals helps to document performance expectations, promote communications, and contribute to the overall employee's development. The format for writing goals are often based on SMART criteria, which are *specific* (describe the results to achieve), *measurable* (clearly written and state a level of achievement expected), *agreed upon* (are agreed upon by the supervisor and employee), *realistic* and *relevant* (are challenging, flexible, and achievable and provide stretch for the employee), and *timely* (are attainable within a specified period of time).

An example of a SMART goal might be "to increase the student achievement performance in the school by 10 percent as measured by the state standards-based achievement test by end of the school year." In addition to having professional SMART goals that are based on the operation of the school, it is common to have *personal development goals*, which are goals that help support the development of the employee. In essence, there are two types of goals, *professional development goals* that are specifically related to achieving the initiatives of the organization and personal development goals that help the employee growth. Examples of these goals for an administrative position include:

Professional Development Goals

1. Reduce student absenteeism by 10 percent by year end.
2. Improve test scores by 5 percent.
3. Develop a strategic community business program.
4. Develop a school crisis management program.
5. Purchase, install, and provide training for using SMART Boards in classrooms.

Personal Development Goals

1. Improve writing skills.
2. Learn a new software program.
3. Improve time management skills.

4. Improve leadership skills.
5. Improve stress management.

Each organization needs to design the performance evaluation system that is best for the organization. Fundamental questions for assessing the evaluation form include "Are the rating factors representative of the job position?" "Is the evaluation form comprehensive but easy to use?" "Is the content fair?" and "Do the employees like the form?" Also, whenever possible it is good to include standards by which each of the performance factors can be measured.

The standards are generally constructed as a rubric that allows each of the levels to be distinguished in giving concrete examples of unsatisfactory, satisfactory, and superior performance. Table 3.2 illustrates a typical performance appraisal rubric listing the standards of performance on a five-point scale. The use of performance appraisal rubrics can substantially improve inter-rater reliability and support objectivity and fairness.

Table 3.2. Performance appraisal rubric listing standards of performance

Job Completion—Quality and quantity of work. Demonstrates accuracy, dependability, punctuality, thoroughness, and timeliness of work in accordance with the job description.

Exceptional: Known within the work unit and across divisions as a person who produces outstanding work. Consistently gets work done ahead of schedule. Adept at conversing with staff and administrators about the best way to approach projects. Work is consistently of superior quality; errors are extremely rare. Performance has contributed to clearly significant improvement in productivity.

Exceeds Expectations: Almost always completes assigned work on time or ahead of deadline. Work is virtually error-free. Rarely needs help or clarification from supervisor. Performance has contributed to fairly significant improvements in productivity and efficiency.

Meets Expectations: Work is usually done on time; sometimes ahead of schedule. Errors are infrequent. Occasionally asks supervisor for help or clarification. Performance has contributed to improvements in productivity.

Needs Improvement: Assigned work is often not completed on time. Work often has errors or is incomplete. Supervisor needs to monitor regularly.

Unacceptable: Assigned work is usually not done on time. Work is usually not complete or has errors. Needs close supervision.

Comments:

Described here are the typical steps for conducting the session.

1. Prepare appraisal form (and schedule logistics for session)
2. Introduce session (set stage, criteria for ratings, and overview of process)
3. Review performance evaluation ratings (for each section of the form)
4. State the overall rating
5. Obtain employee's reaction and discuss developmental areas
6. Obtain employee's signature on form
7. Discuss and agree on next year's goals (optional)
8. Document and file performance evaluation form and information

Every school district should provide sufficient training and guidelines in conducting the performance evaluation for all supervisors. The *preparation for the performance evaluation session* should be thorough, step one. It is important to schedule sufficient time and a location that is private and without distractions.

Generally it is advisable for the employee to complete a self-assessment prior to the session. The employee can either send this self-assessment in advance to the supervisor or bring it to the evaluation session. The advantage of sending the self-assessment in advance allows the supervisor to anticipate the employee's evaluation, although it might bias the supervisor's own rating of the employee.

In step two the supervisor *introduces the session* by providing an overview for the process, establishing expectations, and establishing criteria for ratings and essentially sets the stage for the performance appraisal session. The third step involves the supervisor *reviewing all the performance ratings* for all the sections on the form. Generally, a supervisor reviews each of the ratings and then gives an *overall rating* at the end, step four.

However, it is possible that the supervisor may want to give the overall rating prior to reviewing each of the rating sections. This might be the case when there is an outstanding employee, and giving the overall rating in advance may help to reduce anxiety and allow for a more constructive discussion. When evaluating a poor performer, it is advisable to give the overall rating at the end, so the supervisor can build justification for the rating, especially if the employee needs to be placed on probation.

After the rating has been given, it is often good to obtain the *employee's overall reaction* and then discuss general *development areas*, step five. It is critical to *obtain the signature* of the employee on the performance appraisal form, step six. The signature does not indicate that the employee agrees to the form but acknowledges that the form has been reviewed with the employee.

Also, an optional step in the session might be for the supervisor to *discuss next year's goals* and agree upon the goals with the employee, step seven. In this case the supervisor may request that the employee prepare in advance and bring these goals to the session. However, the best process is one that fits within the culture of the organization and accepted by people.

The performance appraisal session concludes by *documenting and filing all forms* in accordance with district policy, step eight. In the event that follow-up is needed for employees who may be placed on probation, then a schedule would be developed. Most forms are maintained electronically and must be kept secure and confidential.

During the evaluation session the supervisor should exhibit effective communication strategies such as *anticipation, paraphrasing, silence,* and *limit-setting parameters.* For example, the use of *anticipation* is good when dealing with conflict during the session. If the supervisor anticipates that the employee may have a negative response, the supervisor may start by stating, "I know that you have had difficulty with this performance issue in the past, however this is very important to me and I don't mean to disrespect you. However, I would like to hear how you have improved in this area." By using *anticipation* strategy, the supervisor in essence anticipates an employee's potential reaction and tries to reduce the negative feelings that might occur. This can be an effective technique in building positive relationships during the session.

The use of *paraphrasing* is a common communication technique in which the supervisor simply puts in his or her own words what the employee is stating. For example, if the employee states that he or she is having difficulty with classroom management, the supervisor might put in his own words: "So you feel you are having difficulty with controlling student misbehavior, and if so, I will be happy to work with you on this issue." In using this technique, the supervisor effectively paraphrases the employee's statements and reestablishes communication with the employee and validates understanding of the performance issue.

Silence can be one of the most important communication strategies by the supervisor. Often there is a tendency for a supervisor to talk too much and not allow the employee to talk. The evaluation session should be a two-way communication and should allow sufficient time for the employee to provide comments. Never underestimate the power of allowing an employee to do the talking about his or her performance. Also, if the supervisor is slow to speak, the employee may be more inclined to talk and to express comments about his or her performance.

Another technique that can be useful is called *limit-setting parameters.* Essentially this technique provides limitations on the extent in which a supervisor can help support the performance of the employee, especially when the employee is asking for unrealistic support. The supervisor may respond by stating, "I can do this, but I can't do that." This allows the supervisor to negotiate with the employee on support for correcting a performance issue.

However, it should be emphasized that the accountability and responsibility for performance should ultimately be owned by the employee. Keep in mind that limit-setting parameters are a good technique in introducing one's position and beginning the start of resolving performance discrepancies. These techniques can help to ensure accountability for performance and emphasize rewards and consequences for performance.

FEDERAL AND STATE LAWS IMPACTING EVALUATIONS

Critical to the performance appraisal session is adhering to federal, state, and school district laws and policies. There are several laws and potential union contract agreements that need to be understood by supervisors before administering the performance appraisal session. In addition, there may be supportive state and local laws that need to be followed.

Some federal laws may include the *Civil Rights Act of 1964*, which prohibits against discrimination on the basis of race, sex, religion, national origin, color, and certain medical conditions. The supervisor should make sure to restrain from noting any performance that references any of these factors that could be construed as discriminatory.

For example, a supervisor should not rate a female employee lower just because she is pregnant. Another law that may impact the appraisal is the *Age Discrimination Act of 1967*, which prohibits age discrimination beginning at forty. A supervisor should avoid comments such as "Nice job for an old man," or "You need to get with it and get out of the dark ages and learn technology like the young teachers."

Comments like these are not only condescending but may be legally unacceptable. Also, statements regarding people's lifestyle, if irrelevant to the employee's performance or employee code of conduct, should be avoided. Evaluators and school districts need to conduct ongoing training in this area to ensure compliance and avoid the emotional and financial costs that can result when laws are not followed.

Another law that may impact a performance appraisal session is the *Americans with Disabilities Act of 1990*, which prohibits discrimination on the basis of actual, previous, or perceived mental or physical disability. A supervisor should demonstrate caution in rating a disabled employee if reasonable accommodations have not been provided that could have improved his or her performance.

The *Title VII, Section 1604, Sexual Harassment Law* may also apply during the performance appraisal session. A supervisor may genuinely express concern for an employee and may want to show support by giving the employee a hug or by embracing the employee. The supervisor should restrain from touching the employee in any manner other than perhaps a handshake.

For example, upon conclusion of the performance appraisal session, the supervisor should restrain from tapping the employee on the shoulder as a sign of confidence or giving the employee a hug and stating, "I have confidence in you. I know you'll do a great job." The sexual harassment law prohibits "any unwelcome sexual advances or physical conduct of a sexual nature that unreasonably interferes with the individual's work performance or creates an intimidating, hostile, or offensive working environment."

While the supervisor may have good intentions, these types of actions may be construed to be sexual harassment behaviors and should be avoided. The supervisor should be careful in the choice of works and avoid terms such as "honey," "cutie," "good girl," "you're a good boy," or other gender-based statements that could be somewhat belittling and disrespectful and potentially violate sexual harassment laws.

Another federal law that may impact the evaluation session is the *Family Medical Leave Act of 1993*. This law prohibits discrimination against employees who request time off for their own serious illness or a family member's illness. This law may have implications in giving a performance rating to an employee, especially if the rating is less than satisfactory when the performance might have been an approved leave of absence by the employee.

These types of performance issues are not always clear-cut and demand careful thought by the supervisor. Other potential problems may be impacted by union agreement. For example, a contractual agreement may allow an employee to request a third party to be present during an evaluation session, especially when the evaluation is anticipated to be unfavorable to the employee.

SUMMARY

The professional development and evaluation of employees require a systematic and comprehensive knowledge in all aspects of human resource management. Understanding the myriad of state and federal laws and local school policies is critical in managing human resources.

The proper mentoring and professional development of employees can help improve student achievement and contribute to high morale in the organization. Moreover, incorporating an effective performance evaluation system can help ensure that employees perform to the standards required by the organization and allow the school district to remain legally compliant.

There are numerous resources available to assist educators in this entire process and should be utilized to develop the best systems and processes that are relevant for an organization. Moreover, developing a collaborative approach with involvement by all stakeholders can help to ensure agreement and success to the recruiting and professional development programs.

CASE STUDY

You have been recently hired as the school principal for Johnson High School in the northwestern United States. The school has approximately 1,000 students and a teaching faculty that is fairly diverse in age, race, and gender. The academic performance of the students is average as compared to other school districts in the state. There has been significant involvement of one group of parents who do not represent the interests of the entire community. It seems they are more interested in pressuring the school district to hire more women teachers.

The superintendent has also mentioned to you that the performance evaluation system is outdated and that some local area school districts have been using a new computerized appraisal system. He also mentioned that Johnson High School has never had a mentoring program, since it didn't need to hire new employees for several years. Overall, the school board and superintendent have high hopes for you as a new principal.

The school board and superintendent have charged you, as the new principal, to submit five goals and a strategic action plan for the high school for the ensuing school year. Based upon the information in this case, please develop five goals and a strategic action plan.

Exercises and Discussion Questions

1. List the steps and characteristics for developing a comprehensive mentoring program at a school.
2. List and describe some of the relevant federal, state, and school laws and policies impacting the mentoring process.
3. List the characteristics of an effective teacher professional development program and learning frameworks.
4. Outline the types of topics for a typical teacher professional development program.
5. List the five categories and examples for a professional development program.
6. Describe some major reasons for conducting performance evaluations.
7. Describe some of the typical problems in conducting a performance evaluation review session.
8. List and describe some of the pertinent federal and state EEOC laws when conducting a performance evaluation review session.

REFERENCES

Danielson, C. (2007). *Enhancing Professional Practice: A Framework for Teaching.* Alexandria, VA: Association for Supervision and Curriculum Development.

Tomal, D., Wilhite, Robert, Phillips, Barbara, Sims, Paul, and Gibson, Nancy. (2015). *Supervision and Evaluation for Learning and Growth.* Lanham, MD: Rowman & Littlefield Education.

Chapter 4

Leading and Motivating Employees

Objectives

At the conclusion of this chapter you will be able to:

1. Understand principles and theories of leadership (ELCC 1.2, 2.1, 3.1, 5.1, 5.2, 5.2, PSEL 1, 2, 3).
2. Understand principles and theories of motivation (ELCC 3.1, 5.1, PSEL 1, 2, 3).
3. Describe principles of human resource leadership (ELCC 2.1, 5.1, PSEL 1, 3).
4. Apply strategies for leading employees (ELCC 3.3, PSEL 3).
5. Apply strategies for motivating employees (ELCC 3.1, 3.3, 6.1, PSEL 3, 6).

PRINCIPLES OF LEADERSHIP

An effective human resources administrator needs to understand and practice effective leadership and motivation principles and strategies to maximize employee performance. There are many qualities of effective human resources leaders such as technical knowledge, fiscal, interpersonal, training, planning, and coaching skills needed to support the administrative team in achieving the goals of the organization.

One important quality is the ability to establish a clear-cut vision for the human resource function. A vision is a concrete plan that is different than a mission. A mission is a more general statement, and a vision is a more concrete one. Effective HR leaders have the ability to establish a clear-cut human resource vision for the organization that supports both academic and operational performance. They also know how to measure the results of their vision and strategic goals.

Another characteristic of an effective HR leader is that of *role modeling*. HR leaders often serve as the role model for employees and students, and these leaders need to understand and practice good behaviors that support the values of the organization. Good followers often make good leaders. The ability to effectively inspire employees and then to exhibit effective leadership characteristics is critical in modeling these characteristics for employees (Covey, 1991).

LEADING EMPLOYEES

One of the more popular leadership theories that have practical applicability to leading employees was developed by Paul Hersey and Kenneth Blanchard titled *Situational Leadership*. This theory builds upon the situational leadership styles proposed by authors who develop a continuum of leadership behavior ranging from authoritarian to participatory (see figure 4.1).

This theory can be valuable in helping leaders understand the best styles in leading employees.

To understand this theory, there are several terms that need to be defined. Task behavior can be defined as one-way communication (directive behavior) from a supervisor to an employee. When a supervisor uses the task behavior, he or she is giving direct instructions to an employee. The task behavior is very directive, and there is basically no interchange or conversation. In this style, the employee is basically listening to the supervisor.

The term *relationship behavior* can be described as two-way communication between a supervisor and employee. The relationship behavior is very supportive and considers this communication to be a two-way discussion. This behavior also assumes that there is a high emphasis placed upon both talking and listening.

The term *maturity* can be described as the degree of an employee's positive attitude, experience, and overall emotional maturity in performing the job. The maturity level ranges from low, to moderate, to high. If an employee has low maturity, he or she is considered to be immature. A high maturity level would describe an employee as being very mature in his or her attitude and behavior.

In the situational leadership model there are four leadership styles. Style one is called *Telling*. In this style the supervisor uses a high task and a low relationship behavior. This would be an example where the supervisor is giving one-way direction to an employee, and there is virtually no discussion.

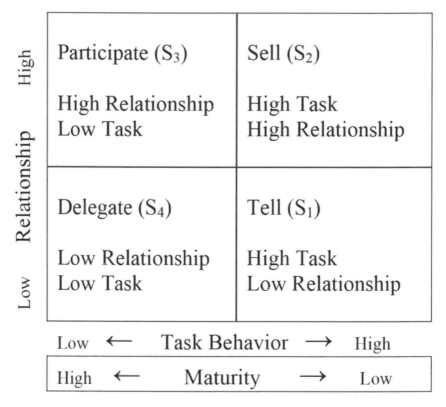

Figure 4.1. Situational Leadership model.

Source: Paul Hersey and Ken Blanchard, 1977.

For instance, a principal could use this style when explaining the job requirements to a new administrative assistant on his or her first day of work.

The second style (S2) is called *Selling*. This style uses high task and high
relationship behaviors. In this style the supervisor is engaging in directive
conversation with an employee. This style considers that the maturity level
of the employee is in between low and moderate. The next leadership style
(S3) is called *Participating*. In this style, the supervisor uses high relationship
and low task behaviors.

This leadership style assumes that the maturity level of the employee is
increasing and ranges between moderate and high. The last leadership style
is called *Delegating* (S4). This style uses low relationship and low task behaviors. It also assumes the maturity level of the employee is high.

Let's examine an example of how a supervisor could use the situational
leadership theory in leading an employee. If a supervisor has a new teacher
assigned to a classroom, it can be assumed that the teacher will most likely
have a low maturity given that he or she does not understand responsibilities

and expectations. In this situation, the supervisor may begin using the style of telling.

The telling style would assume that the teacher knows virtually nothing about the classroom assignment and, therefore, the supervisor would need to exhibit high task and low relationship behaviors. The supervisor would begin by explaining the assignment and expectations while the employee listens. This would be conducted in a personal and professional manner but more directive in style.

There would be no need for two-way discussion given that the teacher initially would not need to have questions versus having the need to gain information. It should not be assumed that the telling style is an ineffective style but can be appropriate for a new teacher who has a very low maturity level. This style is not inappropriate and fits the situation given that the employee is new.

As the teacher begins to mature and starts to understand the assignment and expectations, there becomes a need for both high task and high relationship behavior by the supervisor. In this situation the teacher would use the style of selling. This style assumes that there is two-way conversation with the teacher. For example, the teacher might begin asking questions and participate in conversation with the supervisor, even though the supervisor would still need to be somewhat direct in explaining the assignment and expectations of the job.

As the new teacher continues to mature and develops more of a moderate to high maturity level, the supervisor would then use the style of participating. The participating style assumes that there is a need for high relationship and low task behaviors. In this situation the supervisor needs to continue to give respect to the teacher by embarking in a two-way conversation, and there is little need for the supervisor to be very directive.

As the teacher continues to mature and develops a high maturity level, the supervisor would then use the style of delegating. In this situation there is a need for low relationship and low task behaviors. When the teacher has a high maturity level, the supervisor no longer needs to explain the assignment and expectations of the job because the teacher understands them and is considered very mature.

The example of a new teacher and his or her maturity development provides an effective situation for a supervisor to utilize all four styles of situational leadership in an appropriate manner. While variations may occur in the teacher's maturity level, the supervisor should constantly be aware of assessing this maturity level and adapt his or her style appropriately.

The *situational leadership* model takes in consideration three major aspects—the style of the leader, the employees being led, and the situation. For example, the situational leadership model does not indicate that there is only one right style; rather the model suggests that the supervisor should use the appropriate style given the situation and maturity level of the employees.

For example, if a supervisor observes a staff member engaging in disruptive behavior, the supervisor most likely would resort to the leadership style of telling and would be very directive in asking the staff member to correct the behavior. This style is generally appropriate for communicating with new employees or experienced ones who need more direction or corrective action.

The telling style is often appropriate when a supervisor needs quick directive change in behavior. Another example where the telling style may be appropriate is in the case of an emergency. If there is a fire drill and directive instructions need to be given to all employees for their welfare, the supervisor would use the *telling* style. During an emergency situation, generally there is no need for two-way discussion, but rather the supervisor needs to act decisively in ensuring the safety of all employees and students by giving one-way instruction.

The *selling* leadership style is one that a supervisor may find very useful in needing to convince a staff member to improve his or her performance. When a staff member's performance needs to improve, using the telling style may create resentment, and the *selling* style may be best to establish a professional two-way discussion but at the same time firm and directive.

The *participating* leadership style can be effective when dealing with a staff member who has a moderate to high maturity level. For example, if a supervisor has a staff member who has a negative attitude, the two-way conversation may be the best leadership style. In this situation, the staff member is more apt to accept constructive feedback and improve.

The *delegating* leadership style can be very effective when dealing with a staff member who has a high maturity level. For example, if the staff member is working on a project and is fully capable in completing it, then the supervisor should back off and give the staff member the necessary authority and empowerment. The delegation style can be very effective in allowing high-maturity employees to make decisions without need for much interaction with the supervisor.

The main aspect of using situational leadership includes the notion that the supervisor needs to use the most effective style given the situation. For example, a supervisor may have a staff member who has a high maturity level and has used the delegation style. However, if the staff member begins to lose his or her maturity level and slips to a low level, then the supervisor may need to adjust his or her style accordingly. In this case, if the staff member now has a low maturity level the supervisor may need to adapt the telling style to correct the behavior.

A unique aspect of applying the situational leadership theory is its dynamic aspect. The supervisor may find himself or herself simultaneously using the telling, selling, participating, and delegating styles on a frequent basis. The supervisor may be using one-way directive (telling) behavior with an employee and then immediately switch to a participating style with another. The supervisor's ability to switch the styles quickly is a key in successfully applying this theory.

One danger for a supervisor in using this style is in becoming dependent on using one style too frequently. A supervisor may become trapped in consistently using the telling style, and this style most likely will not be effective in dealing with all employees all the time. Likewise, if the supervisor used only the delegating style, this could have devastating consequences. Employees who need direction may resort to poor performance without the proper leadership style.

One of the landmark theories in developing positive leadership was proposed by Douglas McGregor. He proposed a theory that centers upon the attitude of the leader. He suggested that leaders largely fall into one of two styles—*Theory X* or *Theory Y* (see figure 4.2). McGregor felt that leaders tend to make assumptions about their people. For example, he felt that a Theory X leader assumes that people are lazy, irresponsible, and need to be coerced, controlled, and directed in order for them to perform work. He felt that Theory X leaders view their workers as people who inherently dislike work and have little ambition.

The Theory Y leader exhibits the opposite traits and assumptions than the Theory X leader. The Theory Y leader believes that people are creative, self-directed, desire to work, are responsible, and that work is important to them. Essentially, McGregor felt that the *Theory X* leader is negative and that the *Theory Y* leader is positive toward people.

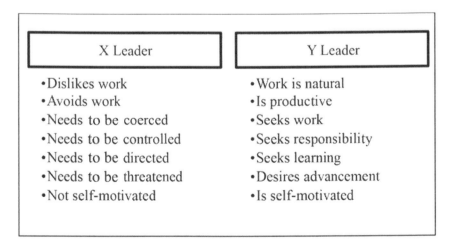

Figure 4.2. Theory X and Y model.
Source: adapted from Douglas McGregor, The Human Side of Enterprise, NY, McGraw-Hill 1960.

McGregor's theory has wide implications for leading employees. For example, if a principal assumes the *Theory X* assumption, then the principal tends to be very directive and threatening to the faculty and staff. The principal often develops a sarcastic attitude. The faculty and staff in turn often behave and perform accordingly. In other words, if you don't expect much, you don't get much. If people are treated as if they are lazy and irresponsible, then they often perform to the leaders' expectations.

While some administrators may not vividly exhibit Theory X behavior, people can often pick up on subtle cues from the leader. If an administrator has tendencies of being a *Theory X* leader, those subtle signs can be observed by people through the gestures. For example, the administrator may have less eye contact with people, exhibit a frown, or the inflection of the administrator's voice can be clues that he or she has negative assumptions about the staff.

Moreover, the subtle use of an administrator's nonverbal behaviors can be revealing. For example, if the administrator tends to point his or her finger and talk in a condescending manner toward the staff, these cues become very obvious and reveal the administrator's true assumptions. It is important to recognize the nonverbal behaviors, since they can sometimes be more revealing than verbal communications.

The *Theory Y* administrator is one who exhibits a positive attitude toward faculty and staff. This administrator promotes a healthy atmosphere and motivates people to perform to their best. The administrator's assumption is to expect the best of the people, and they in turn will often perform to their expectations.

The most important aspect of McGregor's theory is that the assumptions that administrators, as leaders, have toward their faculty and staff can create a *self-fulfilling prophecy*. The notion of the self-fulfilling prophecy is that a belief in an event or expectation can actually cause it to happen. Therefore, if leaders don't expect much from their employees, they will in turn not get much.

On the other hand, if leaders place high expectations on people, then they will often perform to their high expectations. The concept of self-fulfilling prophecy can be seen in many aspects of life. In the sports arena, the concept of the self-fulfilling prophecy is widely used. If a coach places high expectations on his or her players, the players will often perform to those expectations.

For example, if a coach removes a player from the game at a critical moment because he or she does not believe the player can succeed and replaces the player with another player, these expectations can have reinforcing consequences. The player who is removed often will continue to perform less, while the player who the coach has confidence in often improves his or her performance. The essence is that success has reinforcing consequences.

The notion that success breeds success is supportive of the self-fulfilling prophecy. Therefore, whether the leader is a coach leading a sports team or a teacher leading a group of students, the same concepts apply. Essentially, beliefs become reality, and employing these strategies can be powerful motivational factors.

The Leadership Grid

A very popular and classic leadership model is the theory called *The Leadership Grid* by Blake and Mouton (see figure 4.3). The leadership grid describes five different leadership styles. The general notion of this grid implies that all leaders make assumptions regarding concern for production versus concern for people. Concern for *production* implies that leaders have a very high task directive desire for obtaining productivity.

These leaders place higher value on achieving productivity versus concern for people. The left-hand side of the grid describes a scale for *concern for people.* This scale indicates the degree of concern for people by the leader. A low concern for people would be the number one, while a high concern for people would be number nine. In this model the relationship between concern

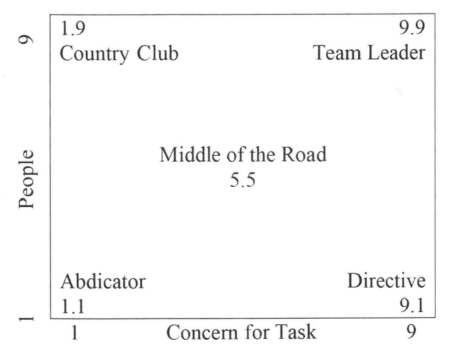

Figure 4.3. The Leadership Grid.

Source: Robert R. Blake and Jane Srygley Mouton, *The Managerial Grid III: The Key to Leadership Excellence,* Gulf Publishing Company, Houston, 1985.

for production and concern for people then can be plotted on the graph. The authors have actually devised instruments that measure a leader's concern for production and people and resultant dominant style.

The *impoverished leader* is one who exerts minimum effort and concern to either people or production. This type of leader can be described as an abdicator. He or she does not have regard for getting work accomplished nor does he or she have much care for the feelings of people. This type of leader can sometimes be viewed as very apathetic and ineffective. For example, if a teacher is suffering from burnout and has negative feelings toward the school system and dislikes his or her students, he or she may adapt the style of the impoverished leader.

This type of administrator may be very resentful toward both the staff and school and is simply waiting out his or her time in order to retire. This type of leader can be very damaging to staff. Generally, this type of leader does not receive much respect, nor does he or she produce a healthy learning environment. The impoverished leader can be described as the one-one manager. This style indicates very low concern for people and production.

The *country club leader* is a manager who is described as the one-nine. This type of leader has a very high concern for people but very low concern for production. This leader is more concerned about satisfying the needs of people than getting results. For example, this type of leader may give exceptionally high performance evaluation ratings to all employees in an effort to gain their favor.

A typical example of this type of leader may be a new principal who desires to have the unconditional support of all of his or her teachers. While this type of leader may succeed in obtaining many friendships, he or she probably does not produce an enriching learning environment. As a consequence, the staff probably will not achieve at their highest level.

Another example of the *country club leader* could be a situation where an administrator has received many complaints from students and community and may feel that his or her job is in jeopardy, so he or she may resort to being overly friendly to the staff without regard to performance. While the *country club leader* may not be as bad as the impoverished leader, nevertheless this style is probably very ineffective in achieving the best results from people.

The *middle of the road leader* can be described as the five-five manager. This type of leader tends to have a balance between wanting to satisfy the needs of people and getting results. This type of leader can sometimes be viewed as straddling the fence because the leader has only moderate concern toward people and production. An example of this leader could be an administrator who simply views his or her job as only a job and places only moderate effort in the concern for people or production.

The *authority-compliance leader* is one who is most interested in getting results and has little regard to satisfy the needs of people. For example, this type of leader would be an administrator who is concerned only with getting high test scores at the expense of jeopardizing teacher relationships. They tend to be very directive and not very friendly toward teachers. While this type of leader is striving to obtain high test scores, the result may be less given his or her authoritarian style.

The *team leader* can be described as the nine-nine manager. This type of leader has a very high concern for people as well as production. The authors believe that this is the ideal style and that all leaders should strive to be the team manager. This style is described as work being accomplished through committed people and that everyone has trust and respect for each other. The authors emphasize that all leaders should strive to obtain the *team leader* style and that this can be a growing process as the leader matures and becomes more experienced.

One leadership model designed specifically for school leaders is called the *leadership capability model* (see figure 4.4). This leadership model illustrates four types of leaders depending upon the degree of the leaders' competence and confidence. In order to understand the model, three terms need to be defined.

Figure 4.4. Teacher Leader Capability model.

Competence refers to the leader's ability to effectively lead and motivate people. High competence indicates the leader's ability to understand both intrinsic and extrinsic motivators and how to effectively use these motivators in motivating people. *Competence* refers to the leader's effectiveness in understanding and applying the effective qualities of leadership and motivation.

The second term, leader *confidence* indicates a leader's feelings of adequacy and self-reliance in leading and motivating people. A leader with high confidence suggests having strong spirit, tenacity, courage, and resolution with his or her ability as a leader. A leader who has low confidence would be apprehensive, having feelings of self-doubt and uncertainty in actually leading and motivating people.

The third term in understanding the model is *self-management. Self-management* refers to the leader's degree of experience, knowledge, and resourcefulness as a leader. Self-management indicates how "seasoned" the leader is in having a good self-concept and belief in his or her abilities as a leader. Self-management goes beyond only being competent or confident and suggests the quality of experience and fortitude in applying both confidence and competence in leadership.

In applying the leadership capability model to leading and motivating school employees, if a leader has low self-management and low competence and confidence, then this leader can be referred to as an *incapable leader*. The incapable leader would have the qualities of not being confident or competent in his or her ability to lead and motivate people. This leader would not have an understanding of leadership and motivational factors and would be ineffective in leading people.

A leader who has not only low self-management but also low competence and a high confidence could be referred to as the *obnoxious leader*. This leader, while having high confidence in leading and motivating people, does not have the competence and therefore may demotivate people. This typical leader is one who is undoubtedly assertive in attempting to lead and motivate people but is ineffective given the lack of knowledge and skills (i.e., competence).

The second type of leader is called the *timid leader*. This is a leader who may have high competence but lacks confidence in effectively leading and motivating people. While this leader may have high self-management in terms of understanding effective strategies for leading and motivating people, the leader is ineffective given his or her lack of confidence.

The fourth type of leader is the *capable leader*. This leader incorporates a high self-management (understands leadership and motivation strategies) and has both high competence and high confidence. This is an effective leader who is able to understand both intrinsic and extrinsic motivators and how to effectively apply them in motivating people given his or her high degree of self-assurance.

The effectiveness of applying this model rests with the understanding that the term *self-management* refers to a leader's understanding of strategies and techniques for leading and motivating people. Being a capable leader not just goes well beyond the understanding of leadership and motivational strategies but also requires the need for high confidence in order to be an effective leader.

For example, if an administrator has a group of employees who are very apathetic and consistently demonstrate poor performance, then the possibility of the leader having both low confidence and competence may exist. This administrator, in essence, may be the incapable leader, and he or she needs to develop high self-management abilities in understanding leadership and motivational strategies and the competence in applying these strategies as well as the self-assurance.

However, an administrator who may be very motivated and self-assured to apply strategies but lacks the actual competence would still have low self-management because of his or her inability to understand the leadership motivation strategies. One needs to recognize motivational factors and confidence levels in understanding the extent to which he or she impacts performance.

On the other hand, the administrator who can be described as the *timid leader* would be one who has a group of employees who may also have performance problems and high motivation. This *timid leader* may be very effective in writing the rules for performance standards but may have difficulty in actually applying the strategies given his or her low confidence. The *capable leader* most likely would have a group of employees who are motivated and have good performance due to his or her ability to communicate the rules and procedures of good performance as well as the skills to apply these strategies in the work setting.

MOTIVATING EMPLOYEES

"You can lead a horse to water but you can't make him drink" is a familiar saying that many leaders can relate to. *Motivation* is a difficult term to define. Essentially it is the willingness of a person to partake in an endeavor in order to satisfy a person's need. Human beings have an innate desire to satisfy basic physiological and psychological needs. Motivation plays a large part in how people satisfy these needs.

Before applying strategies to motivate people, it is worthwhile to first explore what are the factors that can demotivate people. While most people desire to be productive and enjoy their work, various work factors can lead to demotivation, as described here. It is important to recognize which of these factors demotivate, understand the impact on employees, and address them.

1. Routine work that is boring.
2. Inadequate work environment (poor temperature, ventilation, noise level).
3. Excessive supervisory demands.
4. Continuous changes in work and operations.
5. Unequal treatment or perceived favoritism of employees.
6. Personality differences among people that lead to conflict.
7. Outside problems (relationships, financial and health issues).
8. Employee friction and poor morale among employees.
9. Inadequate job standards and work expectations.
10. Inadequate or perceived unequal wages and benefits.

The ability to influence employees to be motivated to have a desire to achieve a goal is an overall objective of educational leaders. While there are many different educational theories regarding motivation, most of them have a common underlying theme regarding the human needs of people. Developing and understanding human needs can be very valuable in motivating employees.

Abraham Maslow (1943) articulated one of the first theories on human needs by classifying them into five different levels. The lower order needs (first two levels) consist of basic physiological needs including safety and security. The higher order needs (upper three levels) consist of belonging and social needs, esteem and status needs, and self-actualization and fulfillment (see figure 4.5).

Maslow's hierarchy can be applied to motivating employees. People may seek different amounts of a certain need than others. Some individuals simply have a higher need for security than other people. For example, many people feel very insecure when living paycheck to paycheck. Some people are greatly affected by not having a savings account, while others feel that as long as they're not in debt everything is fine (i.e., they feel secure).

Likewise, employees may have different need levels. Some employees simply may need more attention than others. Therefore, employees' desire to fill their human needs in the workplace involve a multiplicity of factors such as peer group identification, sense of duty, collaboration, desire for a promotion, attitude toward the school board, and a need for attention and recognition. However, one thing is common: if these needs are not met, the employee's motivation will be affected. Understanding how to meet student human needs can help people to be more motivated and in turn effective.

The two-factor motivation theory proposed by Fredrick Herzberg (1966) is one of the more prominent theories of human motivation. While Herzberg

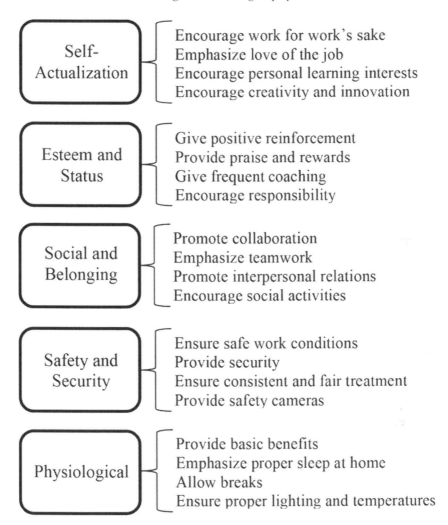

Self-Actualization
- Encourage work for work's sake
- Emphasize love of the job
- Encourage personal learning interests
- Encourage creativity and innovation

Esteem and Status
- Give positive reinforcement
- Provide praise and rewards
- Give frequent coaching
- Encourage responsibility

Social and Belonging
- Promote collaboration
- Emphasize teamwork
- Promote interpersonal relations
- Encourage social activities

Safety and Security
- Ensure safe work conditions
- Provide security
- Ensure consistent and fair treatment
- Provide safety cameras

Physiological
- Provide basic benefits
- Emphasize proper sleep at home
- Allow breaks
- Ensure proper lighting and temperatures

Figure 4.5. Strategies for motivating employees based on human needs.

primarily worked with industrial companies, his theories can also be applied to the education setting (see figure 4.6). Herzberg's model is similar to Maslow's hierarchy and provides a basis for understanding human motivation.

Herzberg concluded that people experience good or bad feelings based upon different types of feelings related to various conditions at work. He theorized that different factors will influence motivation based upon workers' views toward these motivation factors. This research was a landmark study in the field of motivation and sociological needs.

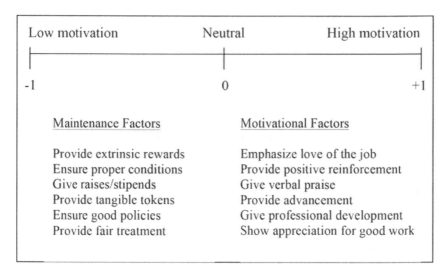

Figure 4.6. Strategies based on Herzberg's Two-Factor Motivation theory.

There were two predominant groups that Herzberg categorized his motivational factors—maintenance factors and motivational factors. Maintenance factors consisted of relationships with supervisors, peer relations, quality of supervision, administrative company policies, work conditions, and reward structures.

The maintenance factors were also called *extrinsic factors*. *Extrinsic factors* can be viewed as external types of rewards that can reinforce performance but are not found within learning itself. For example, an employee may be motivated to accomplish a job task because of the desire for an extrinsic reward such as a bonus. This extrinsic factor, in essence, is the motivator that is stimulating the person to accomplish the task.

Motivational factors consist of work itself, the possibility of growth and advancement, responsibility, status within the organization, recognition, and achievement. Motivational factors can be considered as intrinsic factors. Intrinsic factors are significantly different in that the rewards are not tangible. *Intrinsic factors*, or intangible rewards, are given as a result of the work itself.

For example, an administrator who has a love of education will be motivated in his or her job because of this *intrinsic* satisfaction. For example, in the business world there are often people who are financially successful and could retire, but they would rather continue working because they obtain fulfillment in life. Likewise, teachers who obtain satisfaction from work will be motivated to continue their growth and development and teaching career.

The *two-factor theory of motivation* can be applied to employees in a school. If employee's maintenance factors such as school discipline policies, the administration of the policies, safety and security, and school conditions are not met at a minimum level, employees can become dissatisfied and demotivated. The lack of clear-cut school policies and inconsistent administration of the policies can result in people being demotivated. Likewise, if an employee feels that the principal is ineffective, the employee can also be demotivated.

Much like workers in a company, once *maintenance* factors have been met for employees within a school, in order to provide the opportunity for them to become more motivated, motivational factors must be provided. These intrinsic motivational factors might include potential for growth and learning, peer recognition, awards and work achievement, status within the school, and the rewards of future promotion opportunities. If motivational factors are not provided, employees may never become motivated to grow to higher academic levels.

The *expectancy motivational theory* is another landmark theory proposed by Victor Vroom (1964) that can be applied to the educational setting (see textbox 4.1). Vroom theorized that human motivation is based upon the product of three factors: desire for reward (valence), belief that an effort will result in completion of a task (expectancy), and the knowledge that a reward will be obtained upon completion of the task (instrumentality.)

TEXTBOX 4.1.   THE EXPECTANCY MOTIVATION MODEL

Valence × Expectancy × Instrumentality = Motivation

When applied to the school setting, *valence*, the first factor, can be viewed as a person's preference for receiving a good performance rating (e.g., reward). The person may strongly desire a good rating and will be highly motivated to perform. However, if the person lacks this desire and is indifferent, he or she will have a low valence and will not be motivated to achieve and will consequently lack the motivation.

The second level, *expectancy*, can refer to a person's belief that his or her effort will result in the achievement of a desired task (e.g., successful completion of projects and work assignments). For example, if a person feels that higher quality work will result in a better performance rating, then the person will spend more time on this goal. However, if the person feels there is not a direct relationship between quality work and a positive rating, he or she will be less motivated.

The third level, *instrumentality*, relates to a person's belief that a reward can be realistically obtained. For example, the person might believe that the principal is prejudiced against him or her and no matter how well the person performs quality work, the person will never receive an excellent rating. In this case, the person's instrumentality will be low, and the result will be a low motivation.

Highly motivated employees need to have high levels of all three factors—valence, expectancy, and instrumentality. Vroom theorized that the strength of a person's drive to reach a goal is based upon the combination of these three factors, and a leader should strive to provide incentives for people. Likewise, the experiences employees obtain in the organization can directly contribute to their drive for each of these factors. Leaders can help provide these incentives by establishing work expectations and policies, fair and consistent evaluation, and proper reward structures.

The *equity motivation* model first proposed by Adams (1965) suggests that the motivation of people goes way beyond just satisfying their needs (see textbox 4.2). This model suggests that there is a direct relationship between how employees perform and how they value the rewards. Adams theorized that the issue of fairness applies to all types of rewards such as social, economic, and psychological.

TEXTBOX 4.2.   THE EQUITY MOTIVATION MODEL

Outcomes (compared with others)
- Pay/benefits
- Special rewards
- Psychological

Inputs (compared with others)
- Work effort
- Level of work difficulty
- Performance

The premise of this model is that people will bring input into their work (e.g., personal commitment, time, desire, and energy) and expect to receive outcomes (e.g., money, praise, recognition, and benefits). People will analyze the degree of fairness of receiving their own outcomes as compared to the outcomes being received by others.

The fairness, or equality, of these factors will be subjectively judged by the person. If the person believes that the outcomes (i.e., rewards) justify his or her degree of input as compared with others, then the person will be motivated. However, if the person feels that his or her outcomes are inadequate or unfair as compared to others, then the person will not be motivated (Goleman, 1995).

For example, if an employee is contributing a high input but his or her performance rating is less than satisfactory as compared to his or her peers, an imbalance will result in the employee's perception. As a result, the employee may contribute less input to work. The theory is centered on the notion that employees are constantly comparing their work and rewards with that of the others.

Essentially the *equity motivational* theory explains that the motivation of a person is to avoid experiencing negative feelings that result from unjust treatment. These feelings result from the process of social comparison between people and coworkers. It is important to recognize that the reality of rewards may be different than the perception of the rewards. Employees often perceive rewards being higher to other people than to themselves. The leader should recognize the equity motivation model in motivating people.

While it is important to apply the various theories and strategies on motivation, it is important to recognize that what motivates one person may not motivate another person. In other words, motivational factors can be very individual. Also, what motivates a person at one point in time may not motivate the other person at another point in time. Some of the factors that motivate people are listed here. A useful technique is to review these factors and rank them in terms of importance in motivating yourself and employees:

1. Having a good working environment (work conditions and work hours).
2. Being treated and disciplined fairly by the management.
3. Receiving full appreciation for good performance.
4. Having a great boss who is supportive and reasonable.
5. Feeling as part of the fabric of the organization (feeling connected).
6. Having avenues for promotion and advancement.
7. Having sufficient job security.
8. Engaging in interesting and personally satisfying work.
9. Having a flexible work schedule for personal matters.

While there are many theories and models on leadership and motivation, the topic of *negative leadership dispositions* has not been as widely studied. Based upon the author's consulting work in education and business, an array of *leadership caveat dispositions* has been developed. These dispositions are negative traits and behaviors that the author has observed in leaders. The descriptor "caveat" has been included as a caution to leaders for them to become aware of the dispositions and resist the tendency to fall into the trap of employing them in a habitual manner. There are ten leader caveat dispositions that have been listed and described in textbox 4.3.

**TEXTBOX 4.3.   LEADERSHIP CAVEAT
DISPOSITIONS MODEL**

Disposition	*Characteristic*
1. Need for control	Holds tightly to work reins, decision-making
2. Need to be right	Has an insatiable desire to be correct
3. Need to feel superior	Has very high self-image and self-importance
4. Need to avoid conflict	Avoids confrontations and personal disputes
5. Need to fear rejection	Seeks approval and is overaccommodating
6. Need for controversy	Thrives on drama regardless of consequence
7. Need for affirmation	Seeks acknowledgment and kudos from the team
8. Need to build ego	Displays egocentrism and narcissism
9. Need to feel influential	Desires admiration for personal achievement
10. Need for attention	Seeks to be the main focus and in the spotlight

---

The first disposition is called *need for control*. This disposition is characteristic of the leader who holds tightly to reins of work processes and decision-making. They often need to provide personal input to others' work and give final approval for all matters. Team members often feel undermined, frustrated, and stifled with this type of leader, given they lose much of the freedom and autonomy to do their work. These leaders are often oblivious to their style and team dissatisfaction.

The second disposition is called *need to be right*. These leaders tend to exhibit an insatiable desire to be correct in their decisions. Characteristics of them include they are often highly opinionated, stubborn, closed-minded, and are typically preoccupied with gaining acceptance from others. Team members often avoid giving opinions and challenging these leaders, given they undoubtedly will overrule their employees and be unwilling to compromise.

The third disposition is *need to feel superior*. This leader typically has a high self-image, assertiveness, and a sense of arrogance. He or she may exhibit feelings of high self-importance, competence, and place a higher value of his or her own ability than the ability of the team members. As a consequence, these leaders may tend to consciously or unconsciously belittle their team members.

The *need to avoid conflict* is the fourth disposition. Typical characteristics of this leader include avoiding confrontations, procrastinating, and seeking compromise when in disagreement with others. This type of leader values supportive relationships and cooperation. This leader often fails to make decisions or confronts issues even if it may cause disruption or ill feelings. The result of this disposition is that team members often feel powerless to deal with conflict situations and, therefore, issues often go unresolved.

The *need to fear rejection* is the fifth disposition. This leader typically has a strong desire for individual and group approval. He or she often displays low self-esteem, lacks confidence, and is often seen as being overaccommodating. The leader may become overly dismayed if personal ideas are not accepted by team members. In essence, these leaders want the team members to like them and place a high value on compromising and accommodating in order to maintain high team morale. Therefore, team members may be able to manipulate this leader, given they know he or she avoids group disapproval.

The sixth disposition is called the *need for controversy*. This leader tends to thrive upon drama and suspense in the workplace even if there are negative consequences. This leader may participate in gossip and regularly participates in the organization's communication grapevine. He or she may even purposely instigate interpersonal conflicts to provoke controversy among team members. As a consequence, team members often feel pitted against each other and lack efficiency and productivity.

The *need for affirmation* is the seventh disposition. This leader has a high need for personal acknowledgment and acceptance of his or her actions by the team. He or she typically displays a sense of insecurity and tends to overly collaborate on issues in order to obtain consensus. This leader often seeks personal accolades, kudos, and approval from team members. Therefore, team members may view this leader as lacking strong leadership and as being too indecisive, which stifles team performance.

The eighth disposition is the *need to build ego*. This leader tends to be ego-centered, flirtatious, and somewhat narcissist. He or she often seeks self-admiration, personal loyalty, and praise from team members. If this leader senses a team member is not loyal, he or she may retaliate against the person. With this type of leader, team members typically are guarded in their opinions for fear of upsetting the leader.

The *need to feel influential* is the ninth disposition. This leader typically desires to make a personal difference and be admired for personal achievements. This leader may display charisma, political savviness, and be seen as placing more importance on achieving personal achievement and recognition than accomplishing the mission and goals of the organization. In essence, this leader wants to leave "his or her mark" on everything. As a consequence, team members may feel exploited knowing that the leader's motives are more self-serving than for the team or organization.

The last disposition is the need to be the *center of attention*. This leader desires to be the object of focus and in the spot light—an almost celebrity status. The leader often shows craving for being a topic of interest and values the recognition from being talked about. The need to feel special and to be "set apart" from others is of personal value to this leader. As a consequence, team members may feel persecuted at times by all the leader's attention, which is often at the expense of others.

The first step for any leader is to become aware of these dispositions and to recognize the negative impact they can have on team members and the organization. Leaders may be unaware that they are exhibiting one or more of these dispositions. As a result, they may develop "blind spots" on how their own negative leadership behaviors contribute to inefficiency, low morale, and lack of productivity in the team and organization.

One way to understand whether a leader is displaying any of the dispositions is to complete a personal assessment on the dispositions. The leader can rate each of the dispositions and also ask the team members to rate the leader as well. This probably is best done anonymously to avoid potential for bad feelings and to obtain an unbiased rating by the team members.

Afterward, if the leader identifies any dispositions, he or she should work on overcoming them. The use of professional coaching can assist the leader in recognizing these dispositions, understanding the impact on the organization, and reducing or eliminating them. By avoiding the dispositions, the leader should not only improve his or her own effectiveness but also notice a positive difference in team performance, morale, and organization productivity as well.

The performance of any team is often highly dependent upon the effectiveness of the leader. Good leaders not only should inspire team members for good performance but also need to avoid actually undermining teamwork and productivity through their own unconscious negative dispositions. The effective leader is one who is willing to recognize and eliminate the practice of these negative dispositions.

SUMMARY

The responsibility for supervising and managing employees is a noble one. Human resources directors and supervisors need to understand leadership and motivation theories, principles, and strategies to perform their jobs. Moreover the ability to effectively manage and resolve conflicts and build a collaborative and positive work environment is crucial for effectively operating the school. Also, the job of disciplining and terminating employees is not one to be taken lightly.

There are many legal considerations that must be examined prior to taking action against employees. However, with patience, due diligence, and knowledge of laws and district policies and procedures, human resource directors and school administrators can effectively manage the school.

Becoming aware of these ten leadership caveat dispositions can assist leaders in reflecting upon their own performance and giving insight into areas to improve upon. The understanding of the dispositions can also provide a basis for further understanding leader traits, attitudes, and behaviors that influence the morale and productivity of the workforce.

CASE STUDY

You are a new human resources director at the Wilson Public High School located in the southwestern United States. On the first day of your job the superintendent scheduled a meeting with you to present several human resource issues that currently exist at the school that need to be addressed. The superintendent has asked you to review each of these situations and to submit a report to him as to how you plan to handle each of these issues. The issues are:

1. Employee #1—Henry has been a high school teacher with the district for over thirty years. He has been frequently sick lately, and his absenteeism is becoming a real problem. He has been a good teacher over the years, but lately he seems listless, quiet, and withdrawn.
2. Employee #2—Max is a second-year employee and holds the position of groundskeeper. He is single and he likes to party. In fact, he is often seen showing off his new sports car to others while bragging about his late-night activities. The superintendent has noticed that he often sticks to himself at work and does not perform a thorough job in maintaining the school grounds. He seems to do the minimum job and nothing more. In fact, he has often been seen by the superintendent sleeping during his breaks or coming in at the last minute.
3. Employee #3—Kathy is an intelligent teacher with six years of experience and a high achiever. She finished her master's degree within the first two years of teaching. She is constantly complaining to her colleagues and gives the impression that she doesn't feel motivated or challenged on

the job as before. She also gives the impression that she is impatient with students and bored and frustrated with the job.

4. Employee #4—Mark is assistant superintendent but is deep in debt, which is no surprise to anyone, since he recently purchased a very expensive home, bought a new car, purchased elaborate furnishings, and got married. Since then, the home value has plummeted, and he is "under water" with his mortgage.

He has revealed to the superintendent that he has many college loans and other outstanding bills because of his lavish lifestyle. He has only been an assistant superintendent for about two years, having been promoted fairly rapidly as a young teacher. His wife does not work, and it has been revealed that she is three months pregnant. He already has a three-year-old child from a previous marriage.

It also didn't help matters when the superintendent stated he had overheard Mark talking to a friend in the lounge about his potential gambling problem. As far as his performance, the superintendent feels that he is doing a good job, but lately he seems to be distracted and is having a hard time concentrating and being motivated.

5. Employee #5—Jill is an attractive young administrative assistant who works in the school district office. Unfortunately, she has just filed a sexual harassment claim against John, who is the director of special services for the district. She claims in the complaint that John has sent several sexually based e-mails to her. She also has stated that they used to date but the relationship has soured.

She claims that John is persistent in trying to salvage the relationship. He frequently calls her at her home in the evening. To make matters worse, she has stated that apparently while she was in John's private office he inappropriately embraced her and gave her a kiss, although there were no witnesses. Following the complaint Jill has been irate and has been making inappropriate comments about John and speaking poorly about him to her colleagues and even parents.

Exercises and Discussion Questions

1. Explain the *leadership capability model* that can be used for leading and motivating employees.
2. Explain Maslow's *hierarchy* and how this theory can be used in motivating employees in the school.
3. Describe Herzberg's *two-factor motivation theory* and list several extrinsic (maintenance) factors and intrinsic (motivational) factors.

4. Describe the *equity model* and how it can be used for motivating employees in a school.
5. Explain Tuckman's four stages for team development, and list examples for each stage.
6. List the typical stages in the progressive disciplinary model.
7. List examples of disciplinary offenses that might warrant termination.
8. List and describe at least two EEOC laws that might protect an employee from an illegal termination.
9. Describe the *group think* theory and how this theory could produce negative consequences in group decision-making when terminating an employee.
10. Explain four reasons for disciplining employees.

REFERENCES

Adams, J. (1965). Inequity in social exchange. In L. Berkowitz (ed.), *Advances in experimental psychology*. New York: Academic Press, 267–299.

Alderfer, C. (1969). An empirical test of a new theory of human needs. *Organizational Behavior and Human Performance, 4*, 142–175.

Blake, R. and Mouton, J. (1969). *Building a Dynamic Corporation through Grid Organization.* Reading, MA: Addison-Wesley.

Covey, S. (1991). *Principle-Centered Leadership*. New York: Simon & Schuster.

Goleman, D. (1995). *Emotional Intelligence*. New York: Bantam Books.

Hersy, P. (1994). *The Situational Leader*. New York: Warner Books.

Herzberg, F. (1966). *Work and the Nature of Man*. Cleveland, OH: World Publishing Company.

Kilmann, R. and Thomas, K. (1977). Developing a forced-choice measure of conflict-handling behavior: The "mode" instrument. *Educational and Psychological Measurement, 37*, 309–325.

Maslow, A. (1943). A theory of motivation. *Psychological Review, 50*, 370–396.

McGregor, D. (1960). *The Human Side of Enterprise*. New York: McGraw-Hill Company.

Vroom, V. (1964). *Work and Motivation*. New York: Wiley.

Chapter 5

Building Collaboration and Disciplining Employees

Objectives

At the conclusion of this chapter you will be able to:

1. Understand principles of collaboration and teamwork (ELCC 1.2, 2.1, 3.1, 5.1, 5.2, 5.2, PSEL 1, 2, 3).
2. Understand principles of managing conflict (ELCC 3.1, 5.1, PSEL 1, 2, 3).
3. Apply strategies for building collaboration and teamwork (ELCC 2.1, 5.1, PSEL 1, 3).
4. Apply strategies for managing conflict (ELCC 3.3.3, PSEL 3).
5. Understand principles for disciplining and terminating employees (ELCC 3.1, 3.3, 6.1, PSEL 3, 6).

BUILDING COLLABORATION AND TEAMWORK

Collaboration and teamwork is a critical synergistic characteristic of most organizations. Human resources administrators can play an important role in helping an organization create a positive culture of working together to achieve the vision of the school. While human resources are typically involved with developing policies, rules of conduct, and administering discipline, they can also play a crucial role in building collaboration and teamwork.

Tuckman (1965) identified several stages of team development. Human resources administrators can consider these stages of development in promoting positive teamwork within the organization. The four stages include *forming, storming, conforming,* and *performing.* The *forming* stage can be considered as the honeymoon stage. During this stage, employees are generally guarded, exchange pleasantries, and are somewhat respectful and cordial to each other.

In this first stage, employees are still assessing their environment and the personalities of their coworkers. Employees also experience a degree of uncertainty regarding their relationships with their fellow coworkers and often assess the degree to which they have positive relationships. It is at this stage that relationships begin to develop and the first impressions of people are formed about the organization, culture, and associates.

In the second stage, *storming*, conflicts often emerge, and coworkers may bid for power and rebel against their leader as well as their fellow coworkers in an effort to gain power and recognition. The employees attempt to find their place within the team and a sense of unwritten social order. Employees who emerge as winners often develop informal power and leadership positions within the school.

The third stage is called *conforming* and is sometimes referred to as the *norming* stage. This stage includes employees who establish standards of conduct and set norms for behavior. During this stage, employees for the most part will accept these rules and standards, however, may still lack open support of each other. The team may be very functional at this stage but may lack the full performance potential.

The fourth stage, called the *performing* stage, is when the group is a high-functioning and proficient team. This stage allows group members to feel very supportive of each other, and a sense of loyalty and conflicts are managed constructively. When the leader is able to help a team achieve the highest level of performing, team members feel free to grow and learn and gain new learning experiences. It is at this stage where the group functions most productively and efficiently.

The feelings of employees during this stage are very positive toward each other. People generally have a sense of "we" and collaboration with each other. Much like a good sports team, the feelings toward each of the team members are very cooperative and supportive as they all pursue a common goal (e.g., learning and development).

The leader can help the team members achieve the *performing* stage by identifying clear rules of conduct and a common purpose and by building trust and honesty, commitment, effective communications, appropriate conflict management, and ways of recognition and reward systems. The leader is in essence the person who lays down the tracks and sets the example for the employees to follow. The leader cannot force the employees to become a high-functioning team but can provide situations that allow the employees to achieve high-performance teamwork.

A leader's ability to be proactive versus reactive is critical for all administrators. *Proactive* leadership suggests the leader's ability to anticipate the needs of employees and to take initiative in getting results. The *reactive* leader is one who is content with the status quo and does not have the foresight to anticipate employee needs and creates a working environment that is not vibrant and resourceful. A proactive leader is often one who is also service-oriented. This leader recognizes his or her role as a leader in providing for the needs of others.

The notion of servant leadership is a moral value that entails a disposition of giving and altruism. The assumption that the leader is serving the needs of others is a key feature of moral and ethical leadership (Sergiovanni, 1990). The concept of moral leadership encourages learning that is based on moral and societal redeeming goals.

MANAGING CONFLICT

One of the important aspects in managing employees is the human resources administrator's ability to manage conflict. Human resources administrators often have employees coming into their office with complaints and conflicts with other employees. The leader's ability to effectively manage conflict has a direct relationship with the motivation of employees. There are several sources of conflict in schools. Conflict can result from poor communication, roles, territorial issues, goal incongruence, stress, poor procedures and policies, and ineffective leadership.

The perception or actual favoritism given to employees by supervisors can be a demotivating factor. This perceived or real favoritism is a form of preferential treatment in the eyes of the employee and can lead to disciplinary or performance issues. Administrators often are unaware of the perceived favoritism they may be giving to employees. The perception of favoritism can be as subtle as a mere lack of prolonged eye contact or the inflection of the administrator's voice to certain staff members in a department meeting.

For example, an administrator may be more enthusiastic and positive to some people, which can be perceived as favoritism in the eyes of others. Therefore, administrators need to be aware of their communication and non-verbal behaviors toward all people and ensure that it is done uniformly. When people fail to recognize this, there are often negative consequences in morale and motivation.

The personality differences among students can also be a source of conflict. Employees' personality can be different and can lead to different preferences in approaching team exercises and also can lead to arguments. For example, if employees are working on a project and one employee has a personality of a *doer* and may be more aggressive in wanting to more quickly accomplish the project when working with an employee with the *thinker* personality style.

The *thinker* employee may feel that this employee is being too pushy and short-minded concerning the project. Likewise, the employee's personality style of the *feeler* when working with the *doer* can cause conflict. The *feeler* may perceive the *doer* employee's personality as being insensitive toward him or her. Understanding these personality styles and application to the work place can help in preventing and managing conflict situations in the workplace.

Educators are constantly involved in school change to requirements of state and federal regulations. In addition, demands are often imposed on educators by parents, community members, school board members, and students. These demands, along with the need to constantly change, can cause stress and conflict. Managing change and adapting to change are critical factors to employees. Stability can be the enemy of survival. Change is inevitable, and those who fail to effectively manage change can experience negative consequences.

The school environment can also contribute to conflict. If there is a great deal of noise and stimuli, employees may not adapt well to this environment and conflict may result. The work conditions may be distracting to employees, and his or her ability to focus on work can be hampered. An employee may also be impacted if the temperature of the environment is compromised. For example, if the temperature is either too hot or too cold, employees may have a difficult time focusing on work and begin to displace negative feelings to others.

One of the contributors of conflict is that of miscommunication among people. Human beings are social creatures and communicate on a daily basis. Each of their interactions often involves a negotiating element, which leaves room for miscommunication to take place. For example, if a supervisor makes a statement to an employee and it is misunderstood, the supervisor may have ill feelings toward the person, and conflict can arise.

Likewise, miscommunication can take place among administrators. In addition, there are many forms of communication such as written, verbal, and nonverbal that impact a student's understanding of rules, regulations, and policies. For example, if information is communicated to an employee regarding work policies and procedures, the misinterpretation of the information may have a negative effect upon the person's performance, and conflict can be generated. Likewise, one of the most significant factors impacting upon miscommunication is that of the "grapevine" communication network. There is an informal communication system called the grapevine in schools in which rumors start and contribute to misunderstandings and miscommunication.

Some strategies to help human resources administrators resolve conflict include:

- Understand the root cause and context of the conflict.
- Help people understand that there is more than one viewpoint on a matter.
- Negotiate collaboratively with the parties by examining areas of agreement and disagreement.
- Focus on the conflict issues and avoid attacking the person or becoming emotional.
- Be an active listener and acknowledge the feelings of others.

DISCIPLINING AND TERMINATING EMPLOYEES

Administering discipline to an employee is one of the most uncomfortable and difficult aspects of the supervisor's job. Rarely do supervisors administer discipline without the human resources department being involved. All schools have rules and regulations that must be followed and respected by all employees.

While *discipline* used to be a term that had a negative connotation, many human resources directors strive to implement a corrective action program rather than a punitive one. Most discipline programs are called *progressive discipline* plans and follow a sequence of actions for disciplinary offenses. They are often administered by using a zero tolerance policy with mitigating circumstances considered.

Some factors need to be taken into consideration before administering disciplinary action such as the severity of the offense and if there are mitigating circumstances. Human resources directors must demonstrate due diligence in handling disciplinary offenses. Moreover, many school districts have a union contract that contains specified procedures on handling disciplinary offense.

There is a broad range of misconduct that is prohibited by employees that is special to the school organization. Not only do policies and procedures apply to employees during the normal workday, but given the profession of a teacher the actions of teachers outside the school hours may apply as well. For example, the Internet and social media websites can be used during nonwork hours but relate to work, and employees have a responsibility to follow guidelines often established by school districts.

Also, most school districts take into consideration mitigating or extenuating circumstances for disciplinary offense. These may include the length of employment, past disciplinary record, performance, health issues, attitude of the employee, potential associated disabilities that might have contributed to the offense, and external extenuating factors that might have impacted or contributed to the offense.

Also, many school districts working with the union may classify the offense into groups depending upon the seriousness of the conduct. These groups range from minor disciplinary acts to very serious, repeated, or flagrant acts of misconduct.

Described here are some of the typical employee disciplinary offenses:

1. Wasting time
2. Insubordination; refusal to do a job assignment
3. Improper dress
4. Unsatisfactory work performance
5. Lying to a parent or administrator
6. Possession of a gun on the school premises
7. Using obscene gestures or language
8. Reading a novel while instructing students
9. Falsifying a time card
10. Leaving school without permission
11. Felony conviction while off the job
12. Theft of school property
13. Abusing school equipment
14. Unauthorized soliciting during school hours
15. Oversocializing on the cell phone
16. Bringing alcohol on school property
17. Sleeping on the job
18. Intimidating another coworker
19. Possession or showing sexual magazines
20. Possession of drugs
21. Forgery
22. Harassment of an employee
23. Smoking on school premises
24. Extortion or assault
25. Vandalism or criminal damage
26. Battery
27. Gambling during school hours

When a disciplinary offense has occurred, it is important that the human resources director conduct a thorough investigation. Investigations should utilize scrutiny, analysis, and insight prior to rendering a decision. Some of the reasons why investigations fail include jumping to conclusions, hearing only one side of the problem, failing to be objective, being persuaded by one or two dominant people, failing to follow school policy or union contract, or writing decisions based upon assumptions versus the facts. Table 5.1 shows the steps in conducting a thorough disciplinary investigation.

When taking disciplinary action against an employee there are several considerations that can be taken into account in rendering a decision:

• Punishment or retribution—This generally entails the need to punish the employee for committing a disciplinary offense.
• Deterrents—This factor may be considered to prevent others from engaging in similar conduct.
• Correction or reform—This factor may be considered when necessary to change the attitude or behavior of an employee.

Table 5.1. Steps in rendering disciplinary action

Step	*Description*
Situational analysis, understand disciplinary offense	Obtain background information, get all the facts, isolate behaviors, and pinpoint times and places.
Case analysis—who, what, where, when, and why	Document the facts such as working conditions, equipment that might have been used, job site, hour of the day, witnesses, people involved, motives, emotions, symptoms, and underlying causes that might have contributed to the disciplinary offense.
Summarize the facts	Summarize pertinent information related to the disciplinary incident. Note all special conditions that might have warranted behavior or extenuating circumstances.
Talk to the offender and others	Conduct a disciplinary fact-finding hearing with the offender and all people involved, to document all information.
Render conclusion	Summarize your conclusion as to the offense, mitigating circumstances, offender's past performance, and legal and union considerations, and decide action to take.
Administer the judgment	Hold a meeting with the offender, and render the corrective action after obtaining approval from administration or school board.
Documentation	Document all information, and follow-up in accordance with district policy.

- Legal considerations—This factor may need to be considered to uphold laws that require disciplinary action be taken against an employee for certain offenses.

Most school districts employ a progressive discipline system. The purpose of the progressive discipline is to take a corrective approach in helping the employee understand the performance issue and provide opportunities for improvement. The primary goal is to improve the employee's performance. It is meant to be a fair system that employs substantial documentation and discussion with the employee. In most cases when disciplinary action is rendered, a performance improvement plan should be designed collaboratively with the employee so that the behavior can be corrected. Depending upon the gravity of the offense, the typical stages of progressive discipline in the work place include:

1. Casual counseling
2. Verbal warning
3. Written warning
4. Suspension
5. Termination

The first stage of *progressive discipline* is generally not considered the first formal step in the process. Casual counseling implies the supervisor talking to the employee and providing minor coaching in order to correct a very minor offense. This step can be considered more of a warning to the employee and does not necessarily need to be documented in the human resource file.

Examples could be where a teacher walks into the classroom as the bell is ringing, having grammatical errors in a lesson plan, using of a cell phone during inappropriate times, or displaying a poor attitude toward students. Supervisors need to use discretion when considering whether to administer casual coaching or a verbal warning to an employee for an offense.

The *verbal warning* is technically the first formal stage of the progressive disciplinary program. The verbal warning is followed by a written documentation that is placed in the employee's file. Generally, if the offense or similar offense does not occur within a specified period of time (e.g., one year) based on district policy or union agreements, the employee then reverts back to formal standing.

However, if the same or similar offense is performed by the employee, then generally, depending on the circumstances, a written warning would be administered to the employee and documented in the file. This process would continue until the employee is terminated or reverts to normal standing depending upon the district policy or union agreement. If the behavior leads to termination, the courts consider it to be irremediable.

There are situations depending upon the gravity of a serious offense whereby an employee may be immediately discharged, and all of the preceding stages would be skipped. Examples of terminating an employee based on cause might include indecent exposure, extortion, assault and battery, theft of school property, robbery, arson, engaging in sexual activity, use of severe intimidation, possession of drugs, falsifying school records, forgery, gross civil disobedience, insubordination, rape, cheating or falsifying student test scores, and so on.

Prior to terminating an employee an administrator should always conduct a thorough investigation, consult human resources director, and obtain school board and union approval. Often when an alleged offense has occurred, the employee is sent home with or without pay pending a decision by the school board and administration.

Besides committing an offense, other causes that may result in the termination of an employee may include physical or mental conditions that render the employee unfit to work. There are published federal and state laws on school human resources that administrators need to follow. Moreover, there are generally state, association, and local guidelines and laws that apply.

Some general questions to ask: Did the employer give foreknowledge of consequences of conduct? Was the employer's rule reasonably related to safe operations of the school and expected performance? Was the investigation conducted in a fair and objective manner? Was there substantial evidence that the employee violated the rule and consistently applied to others? And, was the discipline administered reasonable (punishment fit the crime)?

When a tenured teacher is terminated, there are generally specified conditions that must occur during the process. Some of these include formal notification to the employee of the alleged charge and potential action, specified time periods known as statutes and specific termination proceedings that often include a hearing for the charge, school board agreement, opportunity for legal counsel and witnesses, and possible open public forum and recorded hearing.

Some possible actions for dismissal of tenured teachers: Was written notice given to the teacher? Was an offer for a request for hearing given to the teacher? Did the school board notify the state board of education? If a hearing is given, are the hearing officials impartial? And, if the teacher's behavior is remediable, the board should give the teacher a warning in writing stating the specific causes and, if irremediable, may result in further action (including dismissal).

When a teacher is terminated due to cause, the teacher's license may be revoked by the *State Department of Education*. Generally the revocation of a teacher's license is based upon serious conduct such as immorality, negligence of duty, insubordination, incompetence, mental illness, or egregious behavior. One concept that can negatively affect the outcome of a termination decision is called "group think."

Group think, as theorized by Irving Janis (1972) in the book titled *Victims of Group Think*, means that group members can try to minimize conflict and reach consensus without adequately analyzing and providing critical analysis in an effort to strive for unanimity. The term *group think* was first coined by William Whyte in 1952 in a *Fortune Magazine* article.

The symptoms of group think may include illusions of invulnerability, rationalization, stereotyping, self-censorship, direct pressure, and illusions of unanimity among the group members. Essentially, group think is a faulty decision-making process that can occur any time the members of a group need to make a decision, especially when under stress, budgetary constraints, isolation, or time constraints.

Group think may be exasperated when there is a more directive leader and compliant members. Therefore when working as a team to make disciplinary or termination decisions for an employee the group leader should encourage critical evaluators, consider inviting outside experts into the meeting, thoroughly examine alternatives, and encourage independent thoughts and free opinions prior to rendering a group decision (Janis, 1972).

With all disciplinary matters, laws and policies need to be followed prior to rendering disciplinary action or terminating an employee. For example, while drunkenness may be a cause for termination, it is sometimes difficult to prove the frequency of drinking and whether the drunkenness is related to an illness of alcoholism. Health practitioners may consider alcoholism a disease, and the employee may be protected by the Americans with Disabilities Act. Another example might relate to a teacher who is found sleeping on the job.

There are a number of common sleep disorders such as insomnia, hypopnea syndrome, narcolepsy, cataplexy, and dyssomnias. Many of these disorders cause chronic sleeping dysfunction, varying degrees of insomnia, anxiety, and underlying health conditions. Therefore a supervisor should not jump to conclusions in charging the employee for a violation when an underlying medical condition may exist, which would protect him under the Americans with Disabilities Act and other laws.

SUMMARY

All school leaders should be responsible for building collaboration and disciplining employees. Human resources directors and supervisors need to understand the principles, strategies, and current laws and policies in managing people. Moreover the ability to effectively manage and resolve conflicts and build a collaborative and positive work environment is crucial for effectively operating the school.

Also, the job of disciplining and terminating employees is not one to be taken lightly. There are many legal considerations that must be examined prior to taking action against employees. However, with patience, due diligence, and knowledge of laws and district policies and procedures, human resource directors and school administrators can effectively manage the school.

CASE STUDY

You are a new human resources director at the Washington Public Elementary School located in Oregon. On the first day of your job the principal scheduled a meeting with you to present four major human resource issues that currently exist at the school that need to be addressed. She has asked you to review each of these situations and to prepare a report to her as to how you plan to address these issues. The issues are:

1. There is significant conflict among the teachers. Many teachers avoid each other, and there has been open hostility in some of the departments.
2. There is not a defined disciplinary procedure or policy, and the union has been raising this issue for months. The union is threatening a formal charge if not addressed.
3. A maintenance worker was discharged for poor performance a week ago. Several employees feel this was a wrongful discharge and have been protesting. The union is also backing the discharged employee and plans to confront the issue.
4. There are a few teachers who are not performing well. There have been several complaints by other teachers, parents, and students.

Exercises and Discussion Questions

1. Explain the *leadership capability model* that can be used for leading and motivated employees.
2. Explain Maslow's *hierarchy* and Herzberg's two-factor motivation theory and how they can be used in motivating employees in the school.
3. Describe the *equity model* and how it can be used for motivating employees in a school.
4. Explain Tuckman's four stages for team development, and list examples for each stage.

5. List the typical stages in the progressive disciplinary model.
6. List examples of disciplinary offenses that might warrant termination.
7. List and describe at least two EEOC laws that protect employees from discrimination.
8. Describe the *group think* theory and how this theory could produce negative consequences in group decision-making when terminating an employee.
9. Explain four reasons for disciplining tenured and nontenured teachers.

REFERENCES

Janis, I. (1972). *Victims of Group Think.* Boston: Houghton Mifflin Company.
Kilmann, R. and Thomas, K. (1977). Developing a forced-choice measure for conflict-handling behavior: The "mode" instrument. *Educational and Psychological Measurement, 37,* 309–325.
Sergiovanni, T. (1990). *Value-Added Leadership.* San Diego, CA: Harcourt Brace.
Tuckman, B. (1965). Developmental sequence in small groups. *Psychological Bulletin, 63.*

Chapter 6

Benefits and Compensation

Objectives

At the conclusion of the chapter you will be able to:

1. List and describe different types of exempt and nonexempt salary schedules (ELCC 3.1, 3.2, 3.3, PSEL 3).
2. Describe different types of compensation for human resources (ELCC 3.3, PSEL 3).
3. List and describe the various benefits common to human resources (ELCC 3.1, 3.2, 3.3, PSEL 3).

ESTABLISHING A COMPENSATION PLAN

The operation of a school is a big business. Employees need to be compensated for the work they do, and compensation and benefits are the greatest proportion of a school district's budget. It is estimated that over 80 percent of a school board budget is allocated to compensation alone (United States Bureau of Statistics, 2018). With this in mind creating a fair compensation plan can have a great impact on the fiscal health of the organization, recruiting, retention, and motivation of all employees.

Unlike a private corporation, a school district cannot easily generate increased revenue or cut expenses. Many of the costs of running a school are fixed, and the amount of revenue is dependent upon state legislators, the federal government, and local taxpayers. The impact of different types of compensation forms on teacher performance and student learning has been examined for years with much controversy.

The business of public teaching is different than a private business. Educators work with the students they receive and are required to educate them and are not delivering services or producing products for a profit. Therefore, the uniqueness of the role of the school needs to be considered when designing the best compensation plan for a school district.

There are many types of compensation plans used in organizations today. Many school systems use different plans for *classified nonexempt* or *nonclassified exempt* staff. Nonexempt classified staff includes positions such as food services, technology support staff, maintenance and custodians, transportation people, warehouse and distribution, secretaries, purchasing agents, accountants, and school instruction support. These employees often are paid an hourly rate and through the use of a single-rate pay schedule.

Classified nonexempt employees often are paid by this flat-rate approach and differ from exempt positions in that they are allowed by most laws to receive pay for overtime work. Table 6.1 illustrates a typical salary schedule whereby each position is listed with several advancing step positions. The wage amount is often determined by completing a job evaluation. The job evaluation takes into consideration many different aspects such as knowledge and experience, verbal and written skills, job complexity, mental and physical demands, supervisory responsibility, the work environment, and so on.

Many companies and school districts use a point factor system to evaluate each job position based upon predetermined factors in order to build a

Table 6.1. Example of a teacher salary schedule

Year	BA	BA+15	MA	MA+15	MA+30	MA+45
1	$43,000	$45,900	$48,906	$49,560	$51,225	$52,455
2	$46,244	$47,465	$50,583	$51,812	$53,786	$55,018
3	$47,919	$49,250	$53,686	$54,574	$56,349	$57,680
4	$50,137	$51,468	$56,349	$57,680	$59,011	$60,342
5	$52,375	$53,686	$59,111	$60,342	$62,117	$63,004
6	$54,574	$55,905	$61,673	$63,004	$64,779	$66,110
7		$58,123	$64,335	$65,666	$67,541	$68,772
8			$66,997	$68,328	$70l103	$71,434
9			$69,659	$70,990	$72,765	$74,096
10			$72,321	$73,653	$75,427	$76,578
11			$74,987	$76,315	$78,089	$79,421
12			$77,646	$78,977	$80,752	$82,083
13			$80,308	$81,639	$83,514	$84,745
14			$82,970	$84,301	$86,076	$87,851
15			$86,276	$87,407	$89,182	$90,956
Grade	Minimum 20% Below		Midpoint		Maximum 20% Above	

classification structure. In addition, many school district administrators compare their salary schedule with other school districts by conducting a salary survey. Outside employment consulting firms are sometimes used to obtain salary information. The criteria often used to make comparisons include school districts with similar community economic status, household income, number of students, and whether the school is an urban or rural institution.

One of the purposes of conducting a market survey is to create benchmark positions so that the school may decide what percentile of the range they would like to achieve for each of these benchmarks. Often a statistical regression analysis is conducted to create the salary progressions. For example, some schools may desire to be at the 80th percentile of the benchmark. When conducting the market salary survey, comparison of the total compensation package is typically done.

Table 6.2 illustrates many of the benefits of a complete employee compensation program. Other aspects of a market salary survey include pay for holidays, floating holidays, bereavement pay, whether the school district has automatic across-the-board salary increases, merit and bonus plans, wellness programs, employee appreciation programs, incentives for bilingual skills, and so on. The benefits vary from school district to school district depending upon community sentiment, collective bargaining, and school district administration and board.

SALARY STRUCTURES

When establishing the pay for a job position using the job factor system, points are assigned for each of the factors based upon the degree of complexity. For example, table 6.3 illustrates a typical job evaluation form, which tends to be used in business more than in education. In this form an evaluation is completed by the market evaluator through such actions as interviews with existing employees, analysis of comparable job descriptions, review of existing performance appraisal systems, examination of current compensation structures, and so forth.

Table 6.2. Examples of employee benefits

Advanced degree pay	Medical care	Sabbatical leave
Tuition reimburse	Dental care	Personal leave
Shift differential pay	Prescription drugs	Sick leave plan
Cost of living	Vision care	Back pay sick days
Severance pay	Group life insurance	Jury duty
Tax-deferred annuity	Long-term disability	On-call pay
Equipment allowance	Professional liability	Stand-by time pay
Uniform allowances	Pet care program	Commissions

Table 6.3. Job position evaluation with frequency and condition scales

Rate this job by assigning a point value (1–7) for the job activities and work conditions.
Frequency Scale (1–7)

1 = Never
2 = One to three hours per week.
3 = Four to ten hours per week.
4 = Frequent: ten to twenty hours per week.
5 = Very Frequent: twenty to thirty hours per week.
6 = Continuous: thirty to forty hours per week.
7 = Constant: 100 percent of the week.

Physical Work	Frequency
Standing	
Sitting	
Walking	
Running	
Climbing and Lifting	
Stairs or Ladders	
Lifting 0–10 lbs.	
Lifting 11–20 lbs.	
Lifting 21 lbs. or more	
Bending, Squatting	
Repetitive Movement	

Environmental Conditions	Frequency
Using Hazardous Equipment	
Using Equipment	
West Surroundings	
Loud Noises	
High Temperatures	
Poor Ventilation	
Dust or Fumes	
Working Outside	

The purpose of this comprehensive study is to develop a complete and fair compensation program. Based on this information, a modification of the existing compensation system is generally completed. For example, referring to table 6.3, this form illustrates a typical classified nonexempt maintenance position for determining the associated physical and mental job activities and environmental conditions for the position.

The evaluator would actually rate each of the job activities using a scale from one to seven. When completed the total points for each job position is tabulated. Table 6.4 shows an example of a job evaluation tabulation of points for a job factor system. In this example there are seven job factors that are being evaluated. They consist of knowledge; verbal, written, and technology complexity; supervisory responsibility; physical demands; and work conditions.

Table 6.4.   Job evaluation points for job factor system

Job Factor	Director	Manager	Accountant	Clerk
Knowledge	1500	1200	800	500
Verbal complexity	400	400	280	265
Written complexity	300	250	155	130
Technology	300	300	250	150
Supervision	375	150	25	0
Physical demands	30	30	30	30
Work conditions	10	10	10	10
Total points	2915	2340	1550	1085

There are four positions that are being evaluated, which are finance director, assistant finance director, accountant, and payroll clerk. The evaluator assesses each of these job factors per job position and assigns a point value for each of them. The total points are then calculated at the bottom of the form for each of the job positions. The idea behind using a job factor point system is to attempt to establish a fair and just pay schedule based upon the complexity and work conditions of a job.

Many jobs are classified according to a pay grade dependent upon the complexity of each job position. Some administrators assign a pay grade per job title and then aspire to pay each position at the benchmark percentile amount based upon average market data. A midpoint position with pay amounts that are 20 percent below and above the midpoint can also be established (see table 6.5).

This concept implies that a job is only worth so much money. When employees are hired they generally start at the low end and gradually progress to the maximum end of the midpoint range. To achieve higher pay, then the midpoint employees need to produce high performance through superior performance appraisal ratings.

Once an employee reaches the top 20 percent range, typically he or she may not obtain additional merit increases but may be limited to cost-of-living adjustments. The theory of this system is that a job is only worth so much money. If an employee desires to achieve more money, then they need to advance to a higher level through promotion. Table 6.5 illustrates an example of establishing salaries compared to market salaries with 20 percent below and above benchmarks.

Teacher salary schedules tend to utilize the single-salary schedule, which is based upon the concept of a knowledge-based pay structure and education level. The concept is that a teacher should be paid based upon their

Table 6.5. Competitive for 20 percent above and below midpoint

10	$55,348	$69,184	$83,021
11	$59,866	$74,833	$89,799
12	$64,754	$80,942	$97,131
13	$70,040	$87,551	$105,061
14	$75,759	$94,698	$113,638
15	$80,000	$100,000	$120,000

knowledge level for the job. There is an incentive then induced to increase one's knowledge level to increase one's pay. In this system, the teacher would achieve greater pay for each year of employment based upon the level of education. While this type of schedule is fairly common within public schools in the United States, it has been controversial.

Many people feel that this system encourages further education but may have little to do with the actual performance of the teacher or impact on student learning. A teacher may advance in educational level but may not be able to transfer the knowledge to the student's performance. Likewise, a positive correlation may be difficult to establish for length of teaching experience and quality instruction. Just because a teacher has taught for thirty years does not necessarily make the teacher a better educator than one who has taught for five years.

Simply stated, some people might feel that this system rewards teacher employment longevity versus teacher performance. These types of systems have prompted educators to examine alternative forms of compensation that may be fairer and have a more direct impact on achieving performance results.

TYPES OF COMPENSATION PLANS

There are many different types of compensation plans used in organizations today. Some of these consist of profit sharing, gain sharing, merit based, bonus based, noncash recognition programs, deferred compensation, pay for performance, and so on. There is no one best compensation system, and school districts need to establish what works best for their exempt and nonexempt employees. Also, people do not work for pay alone, and other rewards should be considered as part of the entire compensation package.

For example, intrinsic rewards such as having a career progression, job enrichment, the work itself, and full appreciation for the work being done can have significant motivational impact for employees. On the other hand, in the absence of good working conditions, benefits and supervision can demotivate employees as well. All of these factors should be taken into consideration.

In other words simply paying people more money may not guarantee higher performance or good results with student learning (Caillier, 2010).

A report completed by World at Work titled *Compensation Programs and Practices Research, 2010* revealed some interesting statistics:

- There is a wide variety of pay practices and compensation systems, and nine out of ten companies subscribe to a compensation philosophy, with over 61 percent having a written policy and 29 percent having an unwritten policy.
- Forty-two percent of employers indicate that their employees do not understand their company compensation philosophy, and those companies, in which the employees understand the compensation philosophy, believe that a written policy has a positive effect on employees' understanding.
- There is a higher attrition rate associated with companies who have unwritten compensation policies, suggesting that clearly establishing salary schedule and policies has benefits for employee retention.
- Nearly all organizations give a pay increase with a promotion, and award merit increases for good performance. (World at Work Compensation Programs and Practices Research Report, 2010)

The objective of merit compensation plans is to coordinate an employee's performance with their compensation. Many believe that providing merit pay based on performance provides an incentive to perform well and is a fairer compensation structure that may have a more direct impact on quality of work and student learning.

However, determining merit pay requires subjectivity, and these plans are often criticized because of supervisory favoritism, disparities in amounts of money available, poor performance appraisal evaluations, and small differentiations between merit pay and performance. Unless there is a sufficient pool of merit pay to distribute, this plan may create employee dissatisfaction.

For example, if an average performer receives a 2 percent merit pay and an exceptional performer receives a 3 percent pay raise, the difference may not be worth the additional work. Therefore establishing a larger differentiation in merit pay among the levels of performance may be more motivating and fair to employees. Also some compensation experts believe that the merit pay system in itself can produce aggressive competition among employees and undermine collaboration and teamwork.

Employees soon realize that their merit pay is determined based upon their performance as compared to other employees. Also, employees may not be motivated by money alone and may not have a desire to work significantly harder to obtain more money. Some employees may be content with their current pay rate and level of job performance.

A *gain-sharing* compensation program is another option. The idea behind this program serves to reward employees who take responsibility and meet or exceed organizational goals. The program often works when clear organizational goals are established, and employees then strive to meet or exceed these goals. Advantages of this type of program are it helps organizations achieve sustained increases in results, employees have more accountability in achieving organizational goals, they share in the benefits, and there may be enhanced commitment for collaboration and teamwork and school district support.

However there can be many disadvantages to this type of program such as not all employees are able to directly impact the accomplishment of goals, goals are not always easily measured, federal and state Fair Labor Standards Act guidelines may conflict with the plan, and the formulas for determining gain sharing may be complex. However, the combination of gain-sharing plans when constructed in a simplified manner can be beneficial for increasing motivation and productivity in achieving the organizational goals of a school district.

There are several federal and state laws that impact compensation programs. Table 6.6 lists some of the typical laws impacting compensation programs. Many federal and state laws protect employees from employment and compensation discrimination. Human resources administrators need to

Table 6.6. Examples of laws impacting compensation programs

Federal Laws	Description
The Freedom of Information Act, 1966, Amended 1974	Requires government agencies to provide access to compensation information of public schools.
Fair Labor Standards Act, 1938	Provisions for minimum pay, overtime, child labor, and fair compensation for equal work.
Equal Pay Act, 1963	Prohibits discrimination between employees on the basis of sex by paying employees for equal work on jobs performed under similar work conditions.
Civil Rights Act, Title VII, 1964	Prohibits discrimination in compensation on the basis of race, color, religion, national origin, sex, and disability as amended.
Health Insurance Portability and Accountability Act, 1996	Guarantees health insurance to employees and family with preexisting medical conditions.
Age Discrimination in Employment Act, 1967	Prohibits discrimination in employment and compensation for people age forty and above.

proceed with caution and due diligence in constructing fair and nondiscriminatory compensation programs that do not violate federal and state laws and union agreements.

Administering pay raises should be done fairly. Supervisor subjectivity in rating employees, especially for those who are protected class members, needs to be done fairly and nondiscriminatory. Also the ability for the school board to pay given the fiscal condition of the school district can be a daunting task. Since most school district salaries account for over 80 percent of the school budget, any decrease in money can result in the need to terminate employees.

In many states an increase in revenue can only be achieved through successful tax levies which are dependent upon local taxpayer sentiment. State laws regarding operating schools during a fiscal crisis can sometimes supersede local union agreements. For example in times of declining enrollments and decreased state educational funding may mandate reopening of union contractual agreements or institution of reduction in force.

These situations can cause a legal nightmare and significant anxiety to all school stakeholders. Whenever possible school districts should avoid these situations and plan adequately. While this may be easier said than done, alternatives to reopening a contract or a *reduction in force* may be worthwhile such as early retirement incentive plans, hiring freezes, job transfers and consolidations, and a reduction of operating costs.

NONTRADITIONAL TEACHER COMPENSATION

School districts have been experimenting with a variety of nontraditional compensation and incentive systems for the past few decades. While several compensation programs have been implemented, there continues to be controversy regarding their effectiveness (Education Week, 2017). The fundamental reason to employ creative compensation plans is to reward teachers for good performance who get results and support the main goal of the school district—namely improve student learning.

While public school districts are employing more nontraditional compensation programs, charter and private schools have tended to employ these programs. Some of the core questions that need to be addressed include:

1. Do traditional strict salary schedules provide adequate incentives for teacher performance, or do they stifle performance improvement?
2. What is the best way to reward teachers who get results in improving student performance?
3. What are the criteria for determining teacher compensation?

4. Should teachers' compensation be more aligned with corporate pay and incentive structures?
5. Who should decide how much teachers should be paid and at what amounts?
6. Should more emphasis be placed on teacher pay increases and student performance?
7. What other rewards can be given to teachers other than compensation?
8. What are the best intrinsic and extrinsic incentives for teacher performance?
9. Is pay the best motivator for increased teacher performance?

One of the difficulties in implementing nontraditional compensation programs is the element of change. School districts have been accustomed to the traditional fixed salary structures, and any actions to alter these programs are often met with fear and resistance. Teachers may view the nontraditional programs as added responsibilities and more accountability with a lack of control in achieving increased student performance.

As school districts continue to wrestle with developing and implementing the best compensation program, teacher organizations and unions pay close attention to the fairness, quality, and protection of their benefits and compensation. Working together in a collaborative manner is key to all constituents in incorporating the best compensation program that is best for everyone. Without doubt, pay and benefits are a personal and sensitive issue.

There have been a number of nontraditional programs that have been implemented in the United States. For example, the state of Florida has been a leader in implementing nontraditional programs. The state implemented one of the first pay-for-performance programs in 2011. The essential element of the program was the attempt to reward the most effective teachers rather than giving the same pay increase to all teachers independent of their performance.

Another state that has implemented a nontraditional compensation program is Colorado. The program called Professional Compensation for Teachers was implemented as a collective bargaining agreement between the Denver public school district and the teachers' association. Funded by a $25 million tax increase, the program went into effect in 2006 and centered on teacher performance.

Incentives were linked to four categories: academic performance and growth, advanced education, evaluation ratings, and the type of school district. Washington, DC implemented a performance pay system in 2010. This system, called IMPACT, based the compensation on four primary areas: student achievement, instructional expertise, collaboration, and professionalism.

The program was designed to include regular and frequent teacher observations using the school principal and two independent practitioner master teachers. A major element of the program was to link student performance, as measured by test scores, with teacher performance. The intention is to motivate teachers and provide more meaningful reward structures for their performance.

The State of Illinois implemented the Performance Evaluation Reform Act (PERA) on June 13, 2011, with various subsequent amendments. This legislative act outlined the terms and conditions of teacher and principal employment. A major part of this act pertains to teacher compensation, which requires that the evaluation plan provide for the use of student growth has a significant factor. It stated that student growth must be at least 30 percent of the evaluation rating.

The PERA is based upon Danielson's *Framework for Teaching* model and uses a rubric with four performance levels called unsatisfactory, needs improvement, meets performance, and exceeds performance (Danielson, 2007). The use of the performance evaluation form was approved by the state department of education. The PERA has had some resistance given that some teachers feel it is not always fair to rate their performance based upon the students' performance given that student mobility and other factors are beyond their control.

While many states have implemented a variety of teacher compensation programs, most of them have similar features. Table 6.7 describes some of the common teacher compensation and incentive elements. These elements are designed to link teacher performance with value-added factors and scores. The implementation of these programs is dependent upon the collaboration

Table 6.7. Examples of nontraditional teacher compensation programs

Elements	Incentives Linked to Pay	Purpose
Professional Development	Advanced degree certification, License and tuition reimbursement	Promote professional development and knowledge and skills that improve teaching and student performance.
Teacher Performance and Evaluation	Improve attendance Increase student scores Improve teacher evaluations	Promote teacher attendance, teaching performance and student test scores.
Competitive Market	Attract teachers to high-vacancy high-attrition schools and to low-income schools	Promote and attract teachers to high-vacancy, high-attrition, and impoverished schools.
School District Goals	Meet school district goals Meet state and district student performance metrics for goals	Promote incentives for teachers to meet school district goals and state student growth key performance indicators.

and acceptance of all stakeholders such as board members, administrators, teachers, union, and community.

The *Race to the Top* provided a boost to teacher pay-for-performance programs. As part of the initial $4.35 billion competitive grants, states are required to build in evaluations and student performance. The notion was to reward teachers who were highly effective in achieving increased student performance.

The program was also especially directed to high-poverty and high-minority school districts. Several states have been awarded grants, and the program has been instrumental in encouraging all states to revise their teacher compensation programs (United States Department of Education, 2018). Described here are some of the nontraditional school district compensation and benefits programs reported by the United States Department of Education.

Baltimore—Teachers earn salary increases by earning "achievement units" granted through a range of achievements and activities, including professional development, strong evaluations, gains in student learning outcomes, and completion of eligible coursework.

Denver—The Professional Compensation System for Teachers replaces the single- salary schedule with incentive systems. Incentives include schoolwide and classroom student growth, working in hard-to-serve schools and hard-to-staff assignments, skills and knowledge, and earning a satisfactory or better evaluation.

Douglas County—The pay-for-performance programs uses a personal and group development model that leads to recognitions that are financial rewards. The plan begins with desired skills for staff and then cascades to a level of rewarding teacher portfolio and student achievement results.

Helena—The district and union have replaced the single-salary schedule with the Professional Compensation Alternative Program, a compensation system that permits teachers to build salary increases for "positive evaluation, career development and education, and professional service."

Hillsborough County—The contract includes performance pay and "differential pay" for teachers who work in high-poverty schools. The district is moving toward a career ladder under which teachers will be compensated based on three years of value-added student learning gains.

Montgomery County—The district encourages teachers to earn National Board of Professional Teaching Standards (NBPTS) certification by providing specific supports during the certification process and a salary stipend upon achievement of NBPTS certification.

New Haven—The contract calls for the development of a compensation system that includes group-based bonuses. The contract also permits incentives to be offered to exemplary teachers who take on teacher leadership positions.

Plattsburgh—The district offers a flexible spending account to cover the cost of insurance premiums and offers a cash-out option for teachers who decline health insurance.

St. Francis—Placement and advancement on the district's "career lattice" are determined in large part by student performance data, which is based on the specific teacher's assignment and professional goals (United States Department of Education, 2018).

SUMMARY

The compensation of employees for a school district represents approximately 80 percent or more of the school district's total budget. Human resources administrators need to carefully examine all the factors that motivate employees for good performance other than relying only upon pay and benefits. There are many different types of compensation programs that include pay for performance, skills based, knowledge based, gain sharing, and merit plans that can be successfully utilized by the school board.

All these programs should be considered when improving an existing school district compensation program. The school district compensation program, however, can be one of the most important factors for recruiting, retaining, and motivating employees. Therefore the importance of remaining competitive with other school districts is a common goal for human resources administrators. There also many nontraditional teacher compensation and benefits programs, many of which have been initiated as an outgrowth of the United States Department of Education *Race to the Top* initiatives.

CASE STUDY

You are the human resources director for the Kenbar School District and have been charged with totally redesigning the teacher benefits and compensation system. The superintendent and school board have charged you to be creative in developing this new system. They are interested in a modern and leading-edge program that supports teacher accountability and motivation. One board member stated that "we don't want to give teachers raises just because they live and breathe another year—it needs to be based upon performance." Develop this comprehensive proposal with examples. Consider some of these questions in your proposal:

1. Develop a few examples of different benefits and compensation programs.
2. Outline some of the advantages and disadvantages to the programs.

3. Develop a time frame for implementation.
4. What are some of the financial ramifications to the school district for these different compensation programs?

Exercises and Questions

1. Many state pension programs have been underfunded, and this issue is creating fiscal problems. Discuss ways to address this issue.
2. List and describe at least three major federal laws impacting compensation programs.
3. List different benefit programs for employees.
4. Some people feel that the traditional single-salary teacher schedule, based on seniority, is inherently flawed and does not provide motivation for teachers to excel and that other forms of compensation such as merit pay should be considered. Discuss this issue and alternatives for providing teacher incentives.
5. The impact of reducing pay for teachers can be controversial. What are the advantages and disadvantages in doing this?
6. Discuss the relationship between teacher pay and student performance. Does higher teacher pay relate to higher student achievement?
7. Describe some of the features of nontraditional compensations and benefits programs.

REFERENCES

Caillier, J. (2010). Paying teachers according to student achievement: Questions regarding pay-for-performance models in public education. *Clearing House, 83*(2), 58–61. doi:10.1080/00098650903386451.

Danielson, C. (2007). *Enhancing Professional Practice: A Framework for Teaching.* Alexandria, VA: Association for Supervision and Curriculum Development.

Education Week. (3 December 2017). https://www.edweek.org/ew/index.html.

United States Bureau of Statistics. (2018). Washington, DC: United States Federal Government.

United States Department of Education. (2018). Race to the Top Teacher Compensation. https://innovation.ed.gov/teacher-compensation/.

World at Work Compensation and Practices Research. (2010). www.worldatwork.org.

Chapter 7

Unions and Collective Bargaining

Objectives

At the conclusion of the chapter you will be able to:

1. List and describe the different unions in the United States (ELCC 3.1, 3.2, 3.3, PSEL 3).
2. Describe the history of unions in the United States (ELCC 3.1, PSEL 3).
3. Describe different advantages of unions (ELCC 3.3, PSEL 3).
4. List and describe the various disadvantages of unions (ELCC 3.1, 3.2, 3.3, PSEL 3).
5. Describe a typical employee union and school board collective bargaining process (ELCC 6.3, PSEL 3).
6. List and describe various tactics and counter-tactics used in the negotiation process between the school board and union (ELCC 2.2, 6.1, PSEL 3, 6).
7. List and describe the responsibilities of a school negotiation team (ELCC 5.1, PSEL 3).
8. List and describe the major components of the collective bargaining agreement (ELCC 3.3, 5.1, 6.1, PSEL 3, 6).

HISTORY OF LABOR MOVEMENT

The national labor movement in the United States has experienced a long and rich history. The history of organized labor can be traced back to the early 1800s. Local trade unions were formed as a result of many sweatshop conditions that were typical during this era. Many people, especially women, worked in poor environments for long hours; sometimes sixteen hours a day with little breaks and with little pay.

The first union established was called the *United Tailoresses of New York*, which was formed in 1825 by a group of organized women. This early union was successful in achieving better work conditions and pay. One of the earlier large and effective unions was the *Knights of Labor* organized in 1969. This organization led many strikes in railroads, coal mining, and other industries as they strived to improve work conditions and pay.

At times some of these strikes ended in violence and death. Perhaps the most prolific and well-known union was established in 1881 by Samuel Gompers called the *Federation of Organized Trades and Labor Unions*. This organization was active in the formation of trade unions, legislative matters, and child labor rights.

Organized labor and government agencies grew during the 1900s, although they had setbacks in membership due to the Great Depression. In 1932 the *Norris-LaGuardia Anti-Injunction Act* was signed into law, which specified guidelines for joining a union that was signified as a victory for the American federal labor movement.

The *Taft-Hartley Act of 1947* was enacted as a revision to the *Wagner Act*, which included additional restrictions on management and union activity such as union membership, fair labor practices, strike provisions, and collective bargaining agreement guidelines. Perhaps one of the most prominent labor relations agencies established by the federal government was the *National Labor Relations Board* in 1934.

It still exists today and is responsible for the development and administration of many labor acts and provisions governing management and union activities. However, unions have not been exempt from accusations of corruption. The Teamsters Union is one of the most controversial unions and has been accused of labor racketeering and corruption activities (United States Bureau of Labor Statistics, 2018).

Labor unions today have experienced significant decline and represent only approximately 11 percent of the public and private workforce in the United States. Most labor unions are comprised under the parent labor organization called the *American Federation of Labor—Congress of Industrial Organizations*. The change in union membership has declined from a peak of approximately 30 percent to 11 percent and tends to be represented in the construction, transportation, and public employment areas.

In fact almost 40 percent of workers are unionized in public employment work. Union membership for public sector workers represents 36.2 percent as compared to the private sector workers of 6.9 percent. Workers in education and associated occupations have the highest rate of unionization at 37.1 percent. Many of the technology and financial professions, as well as a number of other professions, still tend to be nonunion.

Union membership in education tends to be more associated with states with large urban cities such as Detroit, Chicago, and New York City as compared to southern and southwest states. For example, Texas has only about a quarter of the number of union members as New York, even though there are almost two million more employees. While the union membership has varied over the decades, the patterns of membership have been fairly consistent.

The earnings, as reported by the Bureau of Labor Statistic, indicate that full-time union workers earned a median pay of $917.00 as compared to the weekly median pay of $717.00 for nonunion workers. Variations in this statistics are impacted by occupation, geographical location, size of the organization, and industry (United States Bureau of Labor Statistics, 2018).

The nation's largest education organizations are the *National Education Association* (NEA) and *American Federation of Teachers* (AFT). NEA has approximately three million members and is headquartered in Washington, DC. It also has affiliate organizations in virtually every state and employs over 500 staff members with a budget of over $300 million. The AFT was founded in Chicago in 1916 and represents teachers and paraprofessionals and is the second largest education union representing about 1.5 million members, of which about 250,000 are retired.

In 1998 a proposed merger between the two unions was rejected by the NEA. However the NEA-AFT was successful in forming a partnership in 2000 with the commitment of improving public education and mutual interests although they both continue to operate independently. Although the NEA and AFT have a working partnership, there has been competition between them for membership over the years.

Although the unions have a right to negotiate on behalf of its members, there has been controversy in recent years. Several states have mandatory statutes that govern the rights of public employees to organize and participate in collective bargaining. Some states have taken action to eliminate the collective bargaining rights of unions, especially in the Midwest. Several politicians have run on election campaigns during 2018 for right to work.

For example, the State of Wisconsin, under Governor Scott Walker, officially removed the collective bargaining rights from the majority of state public workers in 2011 and indicated that the state and local government would save $30 million in the budget year. Although his efforts were met with massive protests, opposition, and controversy, he has been reelected, and the state continues to prosper.

There have been public movements in other states to follow similar patterns. In this ruling, a court judge ruled that the decision was unconstitutional. However the State Supreme Court voted 4–3 in favor of the governor. The right for collective bargaining by public workers undoubtedly will continue to be controversial and political. These efforts have continued in other states, especially in the Midwest.

Many school districts, especially private and charger schools, do not have union representation. Some educators believe that if a company or school district treats its employees fairly then there is no need for a union. Some potential advantages for unions include collective bargaining for increased wages and benefits, elimination of disparity in wages, job protection, and improved working conditions.

However some potential disadvantages include higher costs for union membership, limited workplace flexibility, and potential reduction of individual job freedom. Employees of any organization need to decide for themselves whether a union is best for them. The National Labor Relations Act gives the right for employees to organize a union in the workplace.

Employees have the right to participate in meetings, distribute union literature, wear union buttons, circulate and sign petitions, and join together for organization meetings. Also the law protects employees from being threatened or given special promises or favors by employers. This includes but is not limited to pay increases, promotions, increased benefits, or favorable work treatment for opposing unionization. Some of the main causes of unionization include:

- Poor working conditions
- Favoritism or inconsistent treatment of workers
- Employee abuse and unfair treatment
- Inadequate benefits and wages
- Fear of job insecurity
- Compromising health and safety conditions

There are common signs that a union organization drive may be taking place. It is not unusual for union literature to be circulated, union members appear on the premises, rumors begin to circulate, and employees begin to leave the premises for union discussions and gatherings. When a union organization drive begins, management often partakes in a counter-union campaign. During this effort, management needs to be aware of the dos and don'ts of an anti-union campaign.

Some of the actions that are typically allowed by management include:

- Reminding employees of good work conditions, wages, and benefit plans.
- Informing employees that once unionized they may need to collaborate with union officials in order to resolve personal work issues.
- Informing employees that they do not need to talk to union organizers if they don't want to.

- Reminding the employees that once unionized they will need to sign a binding contract between them and the union and must abide by union policies and regulations.
- Notifying employees that they will be obligated to pay union dues if unionized.

There is actually a myriad of actions that are allowed by management during a union drive and just as many actions that are not allowed according to law. For example, some of the unlawful actions by management during a union campaign include:

- Installing surveillance cameras or recording devices in union drive meeting rooms.
- Threatening employees that they will be punished if they join a union or participate in union drive activities.
- Promising employees special wage, benefit, or work conditions if they do not participate in the union drive.
- Discriminating against anyone who is interested in attending union drive activities or meetings.
- Retaliating against any employees who participate in union drive activities.
- Broadcasting to employees that they are not to read any union drive literature, not to wear any union campaign buttons, and that the organization will refuse to cooperate with union if installed.

When employees of an organization desire to form a union, they must complete a representation/certification petition with the *State Labor Relations Board*. For example, the petition needs to be processed through the board's election procedures, and the petitioner needs at least 30 percent of the employees of a given unit to be certified as the exclusive collective bargaining agent for the employees. A typical form includes the name of the employer, employer representative, and name of the petitioning labor organization and affiliation if any.

Other questions include if there is an existing collective bargaining agreement, are any employees currently represented by a labor organization, reason for filing petition, number of employees proposed, and signatures of parties. If the union vote is successful, a form needs to be completed with the Labor Relations Board as well. In addition to these activities there are other forms for decertification petitions, charges against employers for violations, and charges against employee organization or its agents for unlawful practices as well as notice of intent to strike form, all of which need to be filed with the state and/or federal Education Labor Relations Board.

COLLECTIVE BARGAINING AND NEGOTIATING

Fundamentally, courts have indicated that boards of education and unions are required to bargain in good faith. Unfair labor practices result when either party does not bargain in good faith or commits a violation enumerated in codes and contracts. Also, there have been various tests that have been addressed in the courts on what subjects can be bargained. Based upon court rulings, collective bargaining can be classified into three categories: mandatory, prohibitive, and permissive.

Mandatory bargaining includes subjects that relate to an employee's direct work such as wages, hours of work, terms and conditions of employment, hiring, layoffs, and rules of employment. Some judicial tests on mandatory subjects of bargaining include:

- The minimal relation standard, which impinges on or affects in any way a condition of employment or management right.
- The significant relation standard, which includes subjects that are significantly related to a condition of employment.
- The primary relation standard, which indicates if the subject primarily relates to or affects a condition of employment.
- The balancing standard, which is a common test that acknowledges that both sides have significant interests at stake and balance those interests.

Prohibitive bargaining is a category of bargaining that subjects which cannot be bargained for law and are unenforceable as a matter of law. A school board may not unilaterally bargain something that statute indicates in its inherent policy responsibility of management. For example, a right that is protected under state or federal law cannot be bargained away in a contract. Other examples of subjects that are generally prohibitive include:

- Determining the starting day of the school year.
- Decisions regarding the amount of student or instructional contact time required.
- Noninstructional support services agreements.
- Decisions on the use of volunteers in providing school services.
- Decisions on employee group insurance benefit policyholders.

Permissive bargaining is a category of bargaining that includes subjects that are neither mandatory nor prohibitive. They are typically subjects in which the parties can agree to bargain, and the matter cannot be pursued to the point of impasse. Examples include language that is contained in a bargaining contract that cannot be changed unless with mutual agreement or the contract expires, elimination of school programs, issuance or return dates of teacher contracts, and standards of recruiting or hiring processes.

There are a number of different types of bargaining. Some of these include informal discussions, interest-based bargaining, compressed negotiations, and binding arbitration. *Informal discussions* generally include no formal proposal, exchanges of written language that are not legally binding, no regressive bargaining concerns, and absence of any professional negotiations of consultants during the discussions.

Interest-based bargaining (IBB) is different from traditional bargaining in that it focuses on satisfying mutual interests by consensus versus taking one party's side at the expense of the other. It is known by various names such as mutual gains negotiating and win-win negotiating, and generally involves extensive training of the teams in problem-solving and communication techniques. Some characteristics of IBB include:

- Setting ground rules on time and location for negotiating.
- Establishing the roles of all participants and logistics.
- Examining past and existing agreements.
- Mutually establishing goals and expectations.
- Agreeing to participate in IBB training and guidelines.

There are several advantages to IBB negotiating such as open exploration and discussion, mutual concern for all parties, desire for a win-win outcome, and expedited process with time frames. Some of the disadvantages include unrealistic expectations of the parties, need for genuine and collaborative approach, significant time and difficulty in discussions when parties harbor ill feelings, and entrenched hostility.

The process of collective bargaining can be an intense negotiating process. The process often begins with a number of activities such as:

- Reviewing of existing agreements and goals of the negotiation process.
- Establishing the time and location for negotiating and participants to be involved.
- Establishing the roles of participants, procedures for negotiating, and target dates.
- Examining past and present grievances on record by administration or union officials.
- Agreeing to ground rules in negotiations such as video or audio recording, policies on press releases, and impasse procedures.

Compressed bargaining is a form of expedited negotiations, which typically limit the number of subjects and in which proposals are often exchanged prior to discussions, stringent time frames are established, and professional consultants and mediators are often involved, especially when an impasse is reached. *Binding arbitration* is often not recommended to the other types and includes a professional arbitrator to make decisions to prior submitted unresolved subjects.

Typical negotiations involve assembling the school board team, which might consist of the school board president, superintendent, and local school counsel. This team would need to conduct extensive planning and preparation including such items as financial conditions, cost analysis, bargaining issues, work policies, roles of each member (e.g., spokespeople, observer, recorders), and negotiation ground rules.

Likewise, the union representatives would outline their ground rules and bargaining issues. Textbox 7.1 lists some typical bargaining issues between labor and management.

TEXTBOX 7.1.   EXAMPLES OF SCHOOL BOARD AND UNION BARGAINING ISSUES

Salary and benefits	Student discipline and attendance procedures
Teacher professional development	Privacy and leave policies
Professional safety and security	Class size requirements
Extracurricular duties	Work conditions and hours of work
Grievance procedures	Impasse procedures

The negotiation process ideally should be a collaborative win-win process. All parties should demonstrate professional behavior and negotiate in good faith. Some of the positive behaviors in negotiating include:

• Respecting all members and listening to their concerns
• Controlling emotions and remaining calm
• Taking good notes
• Staying alert and being a good participant
• Keeping on the subject and not getting off on tangents
• Being open-minded and cooperative

- Avoiding premature judgments and distractions such as using smartphones and cell phones

During the negotiation process it is not unusual that different tactics and countertactics will occur. Table 7.1 lists examples of negotiation tactics.

While there are many tactics that can be utilized during the negotiating process, it is important to recognize that there are just as many countertactics to these tactics. For example, if one is presented with the *what if* question, the other party might counter this tactic by ignoring the statement and suggesting alternative *what if's* as well. The use of *fait accompli* is an attempt to bring quick closure and agreement to negotiations.

However the other party should use patience and perhaps confront the other party as instigating a ploy to discourage this type of behavior. When faced with the *quick deal*, the party should resist the tendency to give in and perhaps resort to the *forbearance* tactic. Often requesting additional information and being patient may allow the party to discover other insightful information.

Table 7.1. Examples of negotiation tactics and descriptions

Tactic	Description
Emotional tantrum	Exhibiting strong emotions in an attempt to gain control over the other party.
Fait accompli	Presenting a final offer (accomplished fact) in an attempt to bring closure to the negotiations.
Take it or leave it	Making a final offer to the other party in order to close the negotiations.
Good guy–bad guy	Using a combination of a hostile negotiator and a friendly negotiator to gain a competitive advantage.
"What if"	Asking a flurry of questions in order to pry information from the other party.
Dumb is smart—smart is dumb	Asking dumb questions to gain information from the other party that might not otherwise be obtained.
The expert	Bringing in expert testimony or facts and data to convince the other party of your position.
Emotional insulation	Being purposely silent and not responding to create uncomfortable feelings in the other party and gain information.
Deadlock	Playing brinkmanship to increase power and strength to encourage concessions from the party.

   Other tactics that can help a party during negotiations include knowing the facts, figures, and all information that are being negotiated: procedural laws, guidelines, and standards; having total commitment for the negotiating process; becoming as knowledgeable as possible about the process and bargaining issues; taking risks; and developing one's negotiating skills. During the negotiating process, it is good to keep in mind that human beings are social creatures and have similar feelings and aspirations.

   People generally want to be listened to, treated respectfully, give accurate information in good-faith, and avoid uncertainty. Understanding these natural human feelings and behaviors can benefit the negotiator during the collective bargaining process. Moreover, during negotiations it is generally necessary to allow the other party to maintain a positive self-esteem and not to develop an adversarial relationship.

   Every lead negotiator has a style unique to him or her. Table 7.2 lists several styles of negotiating. Understanding the different styles of negotiating can be helpful during the negotiation process. For example, T. Warschaw described six specific negotiating styles, which include *jungle fighters*, *dictators*, *silhouettes*, *big mama–big daddy*, *soothers*, and *win-win negotiators*. The ideal negotiating style is the win-win negotiator.

   This person is objective, nonjudgmental, motivated for collaborative negotiations, and sensitive and open during the process. Ideally this style lacks any liabilities. Each of the other styles of negotiating has assets and liabilities as listed in table 7.2. By becoming aware of one's own style of negotiating and the style of the other party and striving to become the win-win negotiator can help in achieving a successful negotiation.

Table 7.2.   Negotiation styles

Negotiating Style	Characteristics
Jungle Fighters	Creative and charismatic but demeaning and aggressive
Dictators	Assertive, analytical, and shrewd but rigid, demanding, and judgmental
Silhouettes	Discrete, loyal, and tenacious but reclusive, evasive, and uncommunicative
Big Mama–Big Daddy	Caring, nurturing, supporting, and gracious but manipulative, devious, nonrevealing, and overprotective
Soothers	Helpful, attentive, and appreciative but anxious, indecisive, and evasive
Win-Win Negotiators	Objective, nonjudgmental, specific, and open but ideally has no liabilities

Source: Warschaw, T. (1980). *Winning by Negotiation*. New York: McGraw-Hill Book Publishing Company.

Another popular theory of negotiations is called the "principled negotiations model." This model has been described in the book *Getting to Yes* by R. Fisher and W. Ury (the Harvard Negotiation Project, 1981). In this model the authors outline several valuable principles and strategies for reaching agreement in the negotiation process.

Examples of these principles include "goal as agreement, not victory," "be soft on people and hard on the problem," "accept one-sided losses to reach agreement," "view participants as friends versus adversaries" (Ury and Fisher, 1981). This theory of negotiation supports the concept of collaborative negotiations and can serve to help reach consensus.

Another theory that can be helpful in the negotiation process is *emotional intelligence*. Effective negotiators have qualities such as intelligence, ability to persuade people, and emotional intelligence. Emotions play a significant part in the negotiation process. Negotiators can be very intelligent; however, if they lack the emotional skills to deal with people, they might not likely give concessions.

Goldman (1995) articulates five basic competencies necessary for emotionally intelligent people: *self-awareness, self-regulation, self-motivation, empathy*, and *effective relationships. Self-awareness* describes the degree to which a negotiator understands his or her personal feelings (e.g., anger, anxiety, and avoidance) and how these feelings affect one's self during negotiations.

If a person has a high degree of self-awareness, he or she understands what triggers these emotions in himself or herself. The first step in being emotionally intelligent is to understand what sets off one's emotions so that one can be aware of them during the bargaining process. There have been intellectually capable people; however, they lack the ability to control their emotions. Emotions drive decision-making and may produce poor results.

The competency of *self-regulation* describes a person's ability to monitor his or her emotional feelings and be able to regulate them. Once feelings are triggered, the person is then able to employ the necessary skills to control negative behaviors and regulate them in a most productive manner. This may be done through self-talk and self-control.

For example, during the negotiating process if the other party elicits a trigger that produces an emotional reaction, an effective negotiator becomes aware of this trigger and is able to self-regulate this emotion so that he or she does not become distracted. *Self-motivation* is the third competency that describes a person's ability to direct his or her feelings toward a constructive purpose.

All negotiators experience successes and failures during the bargaining process. When a person is able to recognize failures and be realistic and is able to grow and learn from these mistakes, this suggests competence in this self-motivational level. The negotiator's ability to discern between important and unimportant bargaining issues can be critical in this stage. Simply put, some bargaining issues are more important than others, and during the negotiation process concession making is critical.

The *empathy* competency is the fourth level that describes a person's ability to not only recognize and regulate his or her emotions but also to be able to understand how these emotions affect other people. In this stage the person is able to see from another party's perspective and be aware of vulnerabilities. This stage requires the person to be observant and aware of the emotions of others and himself or herself.

The last level of emotional intelligence is that of *effective relationships*. Effective negotiators who are emotionally intelligent must be able to create a humanistic bargaining environment. Essentially at this stage the negotiator is able to separate his or her ego from the bargaining issues. In this way the negotiator can be more objective in dealing with the other party. Developing skills in each of these five competencies can help a negotiator become more successful during the bargaining process.

During the negotiating process the negotiator also needs to develop good communication skills. There are several strategies that can be utilized during the negotiation process. For example, the skilled negotiator might utilize the technique of *paraphrasing*. *Paraphrasing* means to repeat back to the other party in the negotiator's own words exactly what was stated. This helps to reinforce the point that the negotiator is listening to the other party and ensures that the message was understood.

The use of *restatement* is another technique that can be used. *Restatement* means that the negotiator repeats verbatim the other party's statement in an effort to encourage the party to continue talking. The use of *open-ended and closed-ended questions* can also be a valuable technique. Open-ended questions cannot be answered by a simple "yes" or "no" and therefore encourages the other party to continue talking. Open-ended questions usually involve words such as "who," "what," "where," "when," and "how." The use of open-ended questions encourages the seeking of additional facts and information.

Closed-ended questions can be effectively used when the negotiator simply wants to obtain a "yes" or "no" answer. A simple phrase can yield a great bit of information and expedite the negotiation discussion over bargaining issues. *Silence* can be a powerful technique when negotiating between two parties. When faced with silence, people will often talk.

Using moments of silence in a skillful manner by the negotiator can sometimes produce valuable information by allowing the other party to open up discussion and provide information. Silence can also demonstrate that the negotiator is genuinely willing to listen to the other party's concern. The use of *expanders* is a technique of stating simple comments such as "go on," "I understand," and "I see." Expanders encourage the other party to continue talking, and they have reinforcing effect in establishing a negotiating dialog.

The concept of *concession-making* is a critical one during the negotiation process. Good negotiators always allow themselves to negotiate. Some strategies for concession-making include:

- Ask the other party to reveal their demands first.
- Regulate and record all concession-making.
- Seek opinions prior to agreeing to a concession.
- Try to obtain a concession from the other party for every concession given.
- Recognize that concessions are often given at the last minute of deadline for negotiation.

There are many things that can go wrong during a negotiation process, and there are often very high stakes on the table. Not only is there a need to obtain agreement from the other party, but also generally the lead negotiators need to gain approval from their own constituents (e.g., school board or union members). Unfortunately not all negotiations end amicably.

When negotiations reach an impasse, there are federal and state guidelines for proceeding. It is always beneficial for parties to emphasize the benefits for reaching agreement as well as the potential ill effects. In attempting to reach agreement, parties can encourage settlement by discussing the details of the agreement, taking a break or changing the negotiators if deadlock occurs, and maintaining a positive attitude.

Sometimes experienced negotiators like to compare the current negotiating process with past negotiating sessions. In this way the negotiator attempts to bring about consensus and agreement to the bargaining issues. Moreover, skilled negotiators understand how and when to make concessions with the other party. Concession making is a key to achieving successful negotiation outcomes.

REACHING IMPASSE

If an impasse in encountered, some of the common remedies include the use of *mediation* and *arbitration*. Mediation involves securing a mediator to act as a facilitator to attempt to broker agreement between the two parties. Generally this process is not binding and is only an attempt to persuade each party to resolve the bargaining issues.

Arbitration is similar to mediation but generally involves securing a third-party "arbitrator" who will review the overall bargaining issues and render a decision that becomes binding. Arbitrators are professionals who work typically with the various associations and federal and state-affiliated agencies such as the *American Arbitrator Association*.

Often when agreement is reached between the two parties, a ratification vote by the members and the board is necessary. If both parties are able to approve the agreement with their constituents, the agreement is consummated. It is not unusual for one of the parties not to achieve agreement, and they need to go back to the bargaining table for additional rounds of negotiation. It should be noted that the arbitration could be voluntary or compulsory.

Some states utilize compulsory arbitration as determined by state law. Another way to resolve negotiation disputes is through the use of the *Federal Mediation Conciliation Service* (FMCS). This is an agency created by the federal government with the primary goal of promoting labor-management collaboration. The office of this agency is located in Washington, DC, and it contains a list of many arbitrators who are available throughout the country.

The FMCS was created in 1947 and is headquartered in Washington, DC, and has more than seventy field offices. FMCS provides both mediators and arbitrators. When a mediator is used, some of the strategies they provide include reestablishing negotiation ground rules, clarifying issues and disputes, helping parties define problems, keeping the negotiation process moving along, promoting communications and exchange of information, and managing conflict (Federal Mediation Conciliation Service, 2018).

In addition, the FMCS provides a number of different services such as creating annual reports, providing audits of financial statements, performance and accountability reports, annual employee surveys, and congressional matters relevant to labor-management collective bargaining. These services are commonly used by collective bargaining, management, and labor organizations.

Unfortunately, if labor-management negotiations break down, then a strike may occur. A strike is one of the final and deadliest weapons in the union's arsenal that can be used against the Board of Education. However, strikes come with a price and often cause detriment to student learning, employees' loss of pay, disruption in the workplace, community dissatisfaction, and animosity among all school stakeholders.

Generally the State Education Labor Relations Board requires a *notice of intent to strike* for union bargaining units. Therefore, the use of the strike provision should be a last resort. Although going on strike is not always devastating to the organization or the union members and can be just another tactic to reach a collaborative settlement.

Unions often use the strike as a last resort to gain concessions and reach agreement from the school board. It is possible by law that when employees participate in a strike, they may be eligible for termination by the school board for failure to carry out contractual responsibilities.

A specialized type of strike is called the "wildcat" strike. This is a strike that is unauthorized by state legislation and serves the intention of creating a work stoppage by union employees. Regardless of whether the strike is authorized or not it may or may not be announced by union officials prior to striking. Tactical advantages for making an announcement or not can be determined by union leadership.

SUMMARY

The collective bargaining process is of critical importance to a school district. The negotiation process should not be done by unskilled representatives. Skillful negotiators need to thoroughly understand compensation contracts, working conditions, tactics of negotiations, federal and state laws, and the psychology of human interactions.

All these areas can contribute to the success during the collective bargaining process. However, if both parties cannot reach agreement, outside facilitators may need to be secured. Mediators and arbitrators are commonly used to assist in these matters. Both are considered third-party facilitators. Categories of bargaining include mandatory, prohibitive, and permissive. Some types of bargaining include informal discussions, interest-based bargaining, compressed negotiations, and binding arbitration.

Mediation is generally not binding and serves to help the parties reach agreement, while arbitration can either be voluntary or involuntary but often is considered binding in nature. The collective bargaining process should be approached by all parties with good-faith intentions. When both parties utilize a win-win collaborative negotiation process, they are more likely to reach an amicable agreement that best services all stakeholders of the school district.

CASE STUDY

You are the human resources director for the Johnsonville School District and have been charged with leading the upcoming school board union negotiations. The former negotiations between union and management have not gone well. The union has taken a very aggressive and confrontational approach to negotiations. They have invested significant money and outside legal counsel and consultants in an attempt to gain the best contract they can.

The school board is under a lot of pressure to deal with the union and create a more cooperative relationship. In preparation for the upcoming negotiation the school board has requested that you prepare the following:

1. Develop a list of the top six or so bargaining issues that you want to pursue.
2. Create a list of six or so anticipated tactics that may be used against you, and develop countertactics for each of them.
3. Develop a list of several professional behaviors that you feel are conducive for collaborative negotiations.
4. Develop a list of six or more ground rules for undertaking the negotiation process.

Exercises and Discussion Questions

1. Describe the history of unions in the United States.
2. Describe the impact of the emergence of teacher unions in the United States.
3. Media coverage of state and municipal opposition to union bargaining has caused controversy in this country, and some feel that unions are exhibiting too much power and influence, while others feel that unions should have the right to bargain. Discuss this issue and various approaches for resolving this sentiment.
4. Many states and local school districts have encountered severe financial deficits and cannot continue to offer educational programs and extracurricular activities. This situation has also, in some cases, caused hardship for local taxpayers. Discuss ways to deal with this situation.
5. List different teacher union organizations and the history to attempt to merge these organizations into one large union organization. What are the drawbacks to this?
6. The impact of collective bargaining on education has created an adversarial relationship between state government and union members such as the case in the State of Wisconsin. Discuss the ramifications of these situations and provide opinions on addressing this issue.
7. List different unions for classified staff of school districts in the United States.
8. With the increase of charter and private schools, many of these schools do not have collective bargaining or union representation as compared to many public schools. Discuss the fiscal and human resource advantages and disadvantages of these structures and potential impact on student learning.

9. The State of Wisconsin legislation eliminated the collective bargaining rights of some public workers with the state. List the advantages and disadvantages in this decision.
10. List the advantages and disadvantages for having union representation for teachers in a school district.

REFERENCES

Goldman, D. (1995). *Emotional Intelligence*. New York: Bantam Books.

United States Bureau of Statistics. (2018). Washington, DC: United States Federal Government.

Ury, L., and Fisher, R. (1981). *Getting to Yes: Negotiating without Giving In*. New York: Penguin.

Warschaw, T. (1980). *Winning by Negotiations*. New York: McGraw-Hill Book Publishing.

Chapter 8

Managing Human Resources

Objectives

At the conclusion of this chapter you will be able to:

1. Understand the relationship between student achievement and allocating human resources (ELCC 3.3, PSEL 7, 9).
2. Articulate strategies for allocating human resources for higher performance and productivity (ELCC 3.3, 4.3, PSEL 9, 10).
3. Describe the core and noncore functions of a school (ELCC 3.2, PSEL 9).
4. Understand various approaches to identifying efficiencies in a school or school district (ELCC 3.3, PSEL 9).
5. Understand the role of position control in a school district (ELCC 3.3, PSEL 9).
6. Describe the role of technology as it relates to human resources (ELCC 3.3, PSEL 9).

HUMAN RESOURCE CORE COMPETENCIES

Professionals working in a human resources capacity, like all school district leaders, need to possess a set of core competencies to carry out the functions of their work. While there may be differences in the core competencies among district leaders and human resources directors, most cut across all executive leadership roles. While every school district leader need not be an expert in human resources, no leader can do his or her job effectively without a basic knowledge of human resources.

Table 8.1 illustrates the twelve core human resources director competencies (Wilhite et al., 2017). The first one, *school governance*, implies that the human resources director have the skills needed to assist school leadership in working with those groups who oversee the policy decisions of the school district. This may include stakeholders other than board members such as student, staff, and community groups. Activities could include crafting policy, providing professional development, monitoring compliance with state and federal laws impacting the school district, and providing guidance on various employee issues such as bargaining contracts.

Table 8.1. Core competencies of human resources directors

	Core Competencies	Core Competency Descriptions
1.	School governance	Collaborating and working with district school leaders and board members.
2.	School law	Understanding human resource laws impacting district leadership and operations.
3.	Instructional leadership	Being proactive, involved in supporting district leaders and resources in improving district instruction.
4	Resource management	Supporting leadership in human resources and other resources and regulations.
5.	Vision leadership	Working with district leadership in motivating staff for improved performance of school initiatives.
6.	Change leadership	Working with district leadership in supporting and managing school change and improvements.
7.	Communication	Communicating to school district staff and stakeholders.
8.	Strategic planning	Assisting in developing district plans and goals.
9.	School data management	Interpreting and using school data and assessment information for human resource functions.
10.	Community relations	Developing and working with school community members, parents, and so on.
11.	Diverse learner strategies	Providing effective support for diversity and policies impacting instruction for diverse students.
12.	Collaboration	Building collaboration and teamwork.

The second core competency, s*chool law*, is one of the most important ones. It requires the human resources director understand the legal issues impacting human resources and district policies administration and enforcement. While the human resources director doesn't need to have a law degree, he or she needs to have a basic understanding of school law and know how to work with local counsel in applying it to the workplace.

The third core competency, *instructional leadership*, involves supporting the district leadership team in being proactive and engaged in school district improvement of instruction. While primarily the job of the superintendent, the human resources director needs to be involved in helping provide the human capacity to achieve the district instructional goals. This would include recruiting and screening the highest quality staff and designing programs to ensure their continual growth.

The fourth core competency, *resource management*, is a critical one for human resources directors. It involves the managing of financial, facility, and human resource processes and regulations. Without a doubt, school leaders need to be good stewards of taxpayer dollars. They have fiduciary responsibility to manage these resources efficiently and in a responsible manner. This includes managing financial resources for employment and placement, compensation, benefits, and other human resource functions. Since staff costs make up about 80 percent of a school's operating budget, there is no single resource more important. This importance can't be overstated. Entire position control software systems have been created just for this single purpose.

The fifth core competency, *vision leadership*, involves assisting the district leadership team in leading and motivating the staff to achieve school and district improvement goals. While the vision of the school district is the primary responsibility of the school board and district administration, the human resources director needs to play a role in this process as well as develop a vision for the human resources department. People are the greatest asset of the organization, and human resources director is key in not only building capacity for the organization but sustaining it.

The sixth core competency, *change leadership*, includes the leading and managing school and district change initiatives. It is almost a certainty that when there are new initiatives in the school district, they will involve people, and human resources directors will undoubtedly be involved in ensuring that there are right people in the right positions to meet the change. Like all top leadership positions, change and leading change are embedded in the work of the human resources director.

The seventh core competency, *communication*, entails effectively communicating to school district faculty, staff, and stakeholders. The effective human resources director recognizes that communication is continuously evolving and staying on top of current technology and communications systems is critical for the success of the school district. The use of social media, including Facebook, Twitter, and LinkedIn, school district websites, and smartphone technology requires the human resources director to communicate across a wider spectrum of stakeholders than ever before.

The eighth core competency, *strategic planning*, is fundamental to all school district leaders. It involves developing and establishing school district performance goals, human resources department goals, and an entire strategic plan that supports the success of the school district. The process requires skills in conducting organizational surveys, *needs assessment data*, key strategies to accomplish the goals, and metric and key performance indicators. The strategic plan serves as the overarching blueprint for the school district.

The ninth core competency, *school data management*, is common to all school district leaders but unique in many aspects to the human resources director. This core competency requires skills in interpreting and using assessment and other school data to ensure that effective teacher and staff are employed to meet the demands and needs of the school district. Data-driven decision-making is a core process of school leaders, and human resources directors need to use this same process to build the capacity and carry out the functions of the human resources department.

The tenth core competency, *community relations*, involves the entire school leadership team to develop positive relationships and partnerships with the community. To meet this challenge, effective human resources directors need to work with the superintendent to understand the needs of the community and work with the community to incorporate their values, aspirations, and expectations. Involving the community in the school district is one of the keys to a successful organization.

The eleventh core competency, *diverse learner strategies*, is the primary requirement of the academic school leaders but requires the support from the human resources director. This core competency entails assurance of effective instruction for diverse learners. And, one critical area of support for the human resources director is ensuring the capacity of competent employees to achieve educational success for the school district.

The twelfth core competency, *collaboration*, is common to all school leaders. It requires skills in building a collaborative culture across the entire school organization. The human resources director is critical in serving the role of assessing morale and building a culture that supports successful learning. The effective human resources director recognizes that consensus is achieved by good teamwork and working together to support the goals of the organization. The synergism of good teamwork can help create exponential results for the school district.

TEXTBOX 8.1. COMPARISON OF THE CORE COMPETENCIES AND ELLC AND PSEL STANDARDS

School Leader *Core Competencies*	ELLC *Standards*	PSEL *Standards*
School governance	1, 4, 6, 7	1, 4, 5, 7
School law	5, 6, 7	5, 7
Instructional leadership	1, 4, 6, 7	1, 4, 7
Resource management	3, 5, 6, 7	1, 5, 7
Vision leadership	1, 2, 4, 5	1, 4, 5, 6
Change leadership	1, 4, 6	1, 4, 7
Communication	1, 3, 4, 6, 7	1, 4, 7
Strategic planning	1, 2, 4, 6, 7	1, 4, 6, 7
School data management	1, 2, 4, 5, 6	1, 4, 5, 6, 7
Community relations	1, 4, 6, 7	1, 4, 7
Diverse learner strategies	1, 2, 4, 5, 6	1, 4, 5, 6, 7
Collaboration	1, 3, 4, 5, 7	1, 4, 5

These core competencies were originally designed for all school district leaders, especially the superintendent (Wilhite et al., 2017). The competencies were developed based upon the review of literature on leader core competencies. They were also correlated with the standards of *Educational Leadership Constituent Council* and the *Professional Standards for Educational Leaders*. Textbox 8.1 outlines the comparison of the core competencies with these professional standards. The validity of each of the core competencies was correlated with these core standards-based research and expert collaboration (Wilhite et al., 2017).

THE ROLE OF HUMAN RESOURCES IN THE "C-SUITE"

In private industry, the term *c-suite* is used to describe the chief executive officer and his or her cabinet. In secondary schools this is often referred to as the superintendent's cabinet. In either case, the role of the chief human resources officer (CHRO) is not all that different. More and more organizations are recognizing that just having a tactical human resources department is no longer acceptable. The trend is for the human resources department to be proactive and strategic.

What does it mean for a human resources department to be strategic? It means that the focus of human resources must align with the educational strategy of the school district. CHROs must be innovative, research oriented, and know how to sell their organizations in a tightening job market. All organizations are realizing that the key to their success is obtaining and retaining top talent.

With the role of the CHRO becoming more strategic, what skill sets will be critical in the future? First, there will be greater focus on school district branding. That may include using social media, going for university visits, and highlighting school district's culture and pedagogy. Obviously, this has to be in combination with a competitive benefit and compensation plan.

Generation Z is now entering the workplace. We now have four generations of workers: Generation X, Generation Z, millennials, and baby boomers. Each of these generations is looking for something different in the workplace whether it is flexibility, engagement, or benefits. Teacher burnout has always been a challenge for school districts. What types of programs can CHROs create to address these concerns?

An aspect of this shift from tactical to strategic planning is that CHROs need to have a basic understanding of the business functions of the school district. The days of the business and human resources professional running their departments independently are rapidly ending. In fact, one could make the argument that the most efficient and effective school districts in the future will feature high-functioning collaborative business and human resources departments.

WHAT ARE EDUCATIONAL RESOURCES?

Public school leaders across the country appear to be nearing consensus about the necessary characteristics of successful schools. Class size, an advanced college preparatory curriculum, teacher professional development, and differentiated instruction are key factors in helping all students learn. However, implementing these programs is not a cost-neutral endeavor. On the other hand, authors like Stephen Brill note that "if school systems stopped adhering to class size limits now that we know that class size counts less than the quality of the teacher in front of the class" they could invest more in teacher salaries (Brill, 2011).

Educational resources come in many forms. Tying those resources to standards and student outcomes is important not only to have an effective program but an efficient one. What is equally important is how those resources are targeted within a state, school district, and/or school building. The *Every*

Student Succeeds Act (ESSA) raises that bar by requiring districts to budget by school facility. This will allow resources to be tied to teacher quality and student achievement. Table 8.2 shows the pupil-teacher ratio for elementary and secondary schools from 2005 through 2014. Note that the overall ratio has not dropped due to the fact that school districts have not fully recovered from the effects of the 2008 recession.

Schools tend to allocate funds differently than other organizations due to funding constraints, union contracts, and other factors. School educators can define their priorities, but that does not guarantee that the funds can or will be distributed to those areas. In order to assure a proper allocation of resources, the principal should be the responsible party that leads a team in researching the trouble areas of the school to determine whether it is possible to reallocate funds from one area to another. In doing so, the principal has to be mindful of possible school inequities that must be addressed.

Table 8.2. Public elementary and secondary pupil–teacher ratios by selected school characteristics (2005–2014)

Selected School Characteristics	2005	2006	2007	2008	2009	2010	2011	2012	2013	2014
All schools	16.0	15.8	15.7	15.7	16.0	16.4	16.3	16.2	16.3	16.2
Enrollment size of school										
Under 300	12.7	12.7	12.7	12.5	12.6	12.9	12.8	12.7	12.7	12.7
300 to 499	15.0	14.9	15.0	14.8	15.2	15.4	14.5	15.3	15.4	15.3
500 to 999	16.2	15.9	15.9	15.9	16.3	16.7	16.7	16.6	16.7	16.5
1,000 to 1,499	16.9	16.7	16.5	16.5	16.8	17.3	17.1	17.0	17.1	16.9
1,500 or more	18.8	18.6	18.1	18.3	18.7	19.5	19.0	18.8	19.1	19.0
Type										
Regular schools	16.1	15.9	15.8	15.8	16.1	16.5	16.4	16.4	16.5	16.3
Alternative	14.0	14.7	13.5	14.2	14.3	14.8	14.7	14.7	14.3	14.5
Special education	6.2	6.6	7.1	6.8	7.1	6.9	7.1	6.9	6.6	7.0
Vocational	12.0	13.3	11.3	10.7	10.2	11.7	11.8	11.6	11.7	11.8

(Continued)

Table 8.2. (Continued)

Selected School Characteristics	2005	2006	2007	2008	2009	2010	2011	2012	2013	2014
Percentage of students eligible for free or reduced-priced lunch										
25% or less	16.4	16.4	16.3	16.1	16.5	16.9	17.5	16.4	16.4	16.4
26% to 50%	16.1	15.8	15.7	15.7	16.1	16.5	16.2	16.3	16.3	16.2
51% to 75%	15.6	15.3	15.2	15.4	15.8	16.2	15.8	16.1	16.2	16.0
More than 75%	15.5	15.4	15.0	15.1	15.6	16.0	15.5	16.2	16.4	16.4
Level and size										
Elementary schools	15.8	15.6	15.6	15.5	15.9	16.3	16.3	16.3	16.3	16.1
Secondary schools	16.6	16.4	16.3	16.2	16.4	16.8	16.5	16.5	16.6	16.6

Source: U.S. Department of Education, National Center for Education Statistics, Common Core of Data (CCD), "Public Elementary/Secondary School Universe Survey." Table prepared in May 2017.

ALLOCATING RESOURCES FOR HIGHER PERFORMANCE

School administrators including human resources professionals are constantly challenged to meet the academic and socializing goals for the students they educate. Whereas private businesses seek to minimize overhead and increase profits, public schools tend to maximize the utilization of budgets in support of increasing achievement.

In economically challenged times, businesses reduce expenses and increase efficiency to stay in business and attempt to stay profitable. For businesses, productivity is the key. School districts are not used to thinking of productivity on the same terms as private businesses. Schools tend to think of efficiency as simply making "cuts" to balance their budget. However, making certain "cuts" can be counterproductive. Basically, there are only three methods of balancing a school budget: cut spending, increase revenues, or a combination of both.

Unfortunately for most public school districts, the only viable alternative is to cut spending. Spending is the only thing a school district has total control over. Consequently, the key question is with these challenges, how do we allocate resources for higher performance and productivity in public schools?

It is important to remember that in education, about 80 percent of the budget is for personnel and benefits.

Consequently, inputs are heavily dependent on the quality/quantity of staff dedicated to a particular reaching a given outcome, Education Resource Strategies, Inc. (Baroody, 2011) has developed five strategies to help low-performing schools improve their chances for success. Those strategies are:

1. Understand what each school needs.
2. Quantify what each school gets and how it is used.
3. Invest in the most important changes first.
4. Customize the strategy to the school.
5. Change the district, not just the school.

Increasing performance and productivity is dependent on many variables. The key to implementing any plan is to first identify the parameters, needs, and options available. This process should be done in collaboration with staff, taxpayers, and other stakeholders. The second step is to identify the strategies that are available for achieving the outcomes. Outcomes include not only those related to the academic achievement of students but also the fiscal health of the organization. Both these outcomes directly affect human resource allocations and planning.

Class size is probably the biggest driver of educational resources. In a small elementary school with only two sections of each grade level, losing two students per grade probably doesn't mean you're going to have any significant savings. On the other hand, in a large school with multiple sections you may find that you can increase class size by a few students, not affect achievement, and realize staffing reductions and savings. Again, all of this is affected by the composition of the class. In the final analysis, most districts, when faced with budget reductions, will closely guard class sizes as opposed to other nonessential support services.

A number of states have adopted evidence-based state funding formulas to try to allocate funds, in part, based on class size standards and research. Illinois is the latest state to adopt such a standard. Class sizes in the Illinois formula range from fifteen for full-day kindergarten to twenty-five students for core teachers in grades 4 through 12. Included in the Illinois formula are also allocations for specific personnel such as specialist teachers, facilitators, intervention specialists, nurses, aides, librarians, school administrators, and other school site staff. It is imperative that the CHRO be able to interpret the core instructional elements of such formulas, assess their impact on their organization, and strategize how to make use of resources.

Schools and school districts, like most bureaucracies, tend to maintain programs already in existence and have difficulty eliminating those that no longer are effective. Demographics change, as well as best practices and student needs. Confirming educational needs is important in that it forces organizations to reevaluate programs in light of student outcomes. The result of such a process is that resources can be reallocated and realigned to promote both student achievement and teacher quality in a productive and efficient manner.

Care should be exercised to comply with all legal requirements. Most categorical programs such as special education, response to intervention (RTI), and bilingual programs have specific requirements set, but the state RTI, which focuses on research-based interventions and instruction for general education students, has been adopted by a growing number of states in America (Zirkel, 2011). RTI, which focuses primarily on reading improvement, may hold the promise of reducing costs by implementing early interventions.

There are several strategies to confirm an organization's current instructional needs. Among these are reviewing information that will shed light on which practices, programs, and policies have been effective and produced measurable improvements in student achievement and/or outcomes. Simply put, invest in what works. This is especially important in times of limited educational resources. Shifting resources from less effective to more effective programs and strategies will most likely result in the least amount of harm to students.

A part of the process of confirming educational needs requires that new courses, programs, and instructional strategies contain a fiscal analysis or business plan. Educators need to commit the organization to evaluating new initiatives from both an instructional and fiscal basis. Also, educators need to determine if there is evidence that the results achieved are cost-effective or if the resources designated for the new initiative could be better spent on investing in current programs and services.

Often educators just look at the cost of staff and textbooks. A better approach would be to include all costs: staff, benefits, professional development, supplies, textbooks, equipment, digital materials, facilities, and so forth. How many students will the initiative serve? Will there be a need for indirect resources such as counselors, media specialists, technologists, and so forth.

Schools and school districts can utilize a more structured and systematic approach to confirming instructional needs by comparing programs and functions within their system on several levels—priority, impact on achievement, and cost. Basically, it involves reviewing and evaluating programs on their effectiveness. Program plans are submitted at various funding levels outlining expected outcomes, activities, and evaluation techniques at each level. Once all the data are acquired, programs are then ranked based on whether they should be reduced, stay the same, or receive more resources.

The most recent development is the Government Finance Officers Association's (GFOA) *Smarter School Spending* framework. The framework provides a blueprint for analyzing student learning, setting instructional priorities, and then making the connection between the priorities and finances. The key components of the GFOA framework are:

1. Plan and prepare
2. Set instructional priorities
3. Pay for priorities
4. Implement plan
5. Ensure stability

The GFOA site is free, and they provide templates to assist school districts in not only analyzing where they are but also where they want to go.

The primary purpose of schools and school systems is to educate children. In accomplishing that purpose, a number of services are necessary that have nothing to do with student achievement or outcomes. Those services could be referred to as noncore functions of the school as opposed to the core competencies of academic preparation.

In private industry, if a function is not generating a profit, it is usually considered a noncore function, and organizations seek to look for the most efficient ways of providing the service. In schools and school districts, the noncore functions might include student transportation services, custodial and maintenance services, food service, security, and other similar auxiliary services.

Not all states allow for the outsourcing of these services or have passed stringent rules protecting work done by union employees from arbitrarily being outsourced. However, in states where outsourcing is legal it can lead to substantial savings in these noncore functions.

Whether these services are provided internally or externally, they should be reviewed periodically to ensure they are being provided in the most efficient and cost-effective manner. Schools and school districts need to adopt an entrepreneurial mind-set in this regard. They need to ask four key questions:

1. Why am I doing this?
2. If I don't do this, what's the consequence?
3. Can somebody else do it better?
4. Is it a core competency?

The key to managing staff efficiently and effectively is to have an effective position control system. Simply, a position control system defines every position within an organization, attaches every employee to a specific position, and then tracks all costs associated with these positions including vacancies. Why is this important? Approximately 75 to 85 percent of all school district expenditures are associated with human resource costs—salary and benefits. Position control system can help improve fiscal efficiency and serve to:

• Assist with staff planning and hiring, budgetary control, and position monitoring;
• Ensure staff are assigned only to authorized positions;
• Eliminate payments to staff that are not authorized in the budget;
• Provide accountability by department and activity for positions hired, maintained, and funded.

An effective position control system creates checks and balances between personnel decisions and budgets. It ensures the position is not only authorized but is available, has funding, and is assigned to the correct account. Position control systems are especially useful tools in human resource forecasting. Defining a position includes not only compensation but also benefits, work week/year, leave entitlements, and other contractual benefits.

Process mapping is another strategy that can be used to streamline operations and increase efficiency. A process map defines how an organization performs work, what are the steps and sequence involved, who is responsible for each step, and how various groups interact. One Gartner study suggests that the simple exercise of getting employees together to jointly map their processes, with no subsequent process improvement efforts, can result in productivity improvements of 12 percent or more. Figure 8.1 shows an example of a process map for a school district's business function.

Figure 8.2 shows the purchasing process after it was revised. Notice how many fewer steps there are in the process. This results in both efficiency and productivity gains by just changing "how things are done." In other words, the organization may need fewer staff to perform the tasks, or the time saved may be repurposed for other tasks.

Process mapping can also be useful to:

1. Document and map existing human resource practices including, but not limited to, hiring and replacing positions, changing hours and/or funding of positions, and payroll-related issues.
2. Outline key practices that may hinder internal workflow, data-based decision-making, authorization, and management of personnel-related activities.

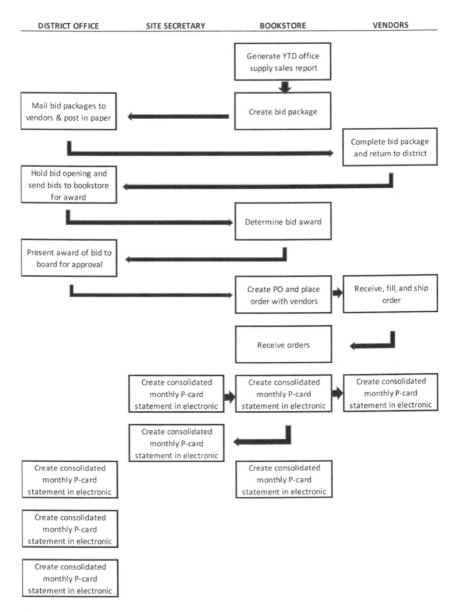

Figure 8.1. Example of process mapping.

| DISTRICT OFFICE | SITE SECRETARY | BOOKSTORE | VENDORS |

Create standing PO to encumber money

Place online order before last day of school

Receive order and package delivery 2 weeks before school

Receive order packaged with teacher name

Create consolidated monthly P-card statement in electronic

Upload P-card statement into finance system

Figure 8.2. Example of the final online process map for purchasing.

3. Provide recommendations for minimizing and/or eliminating duplicate activities, streamlining work functions, minimizing errors, enhancing productivity, and eliminating non-value-added activity (e.g., multiple recording of data).

Common sense would tell us that we should pay only for what we need. Practically, however, this is not always the case. Many school districts consider a full-time employee to be working 8 hours per day for 260 days, or 2,080 hours per year. The following example shows how just a small change in those contracts can result in substantial savings.

Before: The district has 100 secretaries working eight hours per day for 260 days. Those secretaries are entitled to an average of fifteen holidays and ten days of vacation. They are scheduled for winter and spring break. The average salary is $30,000 per year. Total cost to the school district: $30,000 × 100 = $3,000,000.

After: The district identifies a core of twenty secretarial positions that need to work full-time over the winter and spring breaks and during the summer. For the remaining positions the district eliminates work over the winter break (ten days), spring break (five days), and during the summer these positions work only a four-day work week for eight weeks (eight days).

The result is that staff will work only when they are needed. The district can also possibly negotiate or reduce the amount of vacation time since the staff will be off the equivalent of about five weeks.

Furthermore, the district could implement the change as positions open. Total cost to the school district after changes: $30,000 × 20 = $600,000, plus $27,346 times 80 = $2,187,680 for a total of $2,787,680—an annual savings of $212,320 or 7 percent.

Human resource audits can be performed internally or with the help of an outside consulting firm. A human resource audit can be used to review specific practices or simply define positions and compensation levels. A full personnel or human resource audit would include identifying personnel demographics including number of positions, salary and tenure, compliance with personnel record-keeping, compliance with federal and state laws, employment and recruiting practices, evaluation processes, and job descriptions.

As noted previously, human resource audits can also be used to identify processes, practices, and compensation levels. When used in this manner, this audit can result in efficiencies through workflow analysis and alignment of positions and compensation. The following example is one such approach to conducting this type of audit for a clerical staff:

- Develop a bank of questions (tasks) for the clerical staff and department focus groups to procure feedback. Focus groups would include administrators only, clerical staff only, and cross-sectional groups that would include both administrative and clerical staff. Examples of questions would include the following: What percentage of the time do you spend interacting with students each day? Who are your customers? What tasks performed by administrators could be performed by clerical staff?
- Identify and distribute a list of tasks to all staff and ask them to identify the frequency that the tasks are performed (daily, weekly, monthly, etc.)
- Identify the appropriate job classifications used by the U.S. Department of Labor as opposed to traditional school categories. This allows for regional, state, and national comparisons, as well as standardized categories and job descriptions. For a clerical staff the categories might include executive secretaries and administrative assistants, secretaries, bookkeepers, accounting and auditing clerks, and receptionist and information clerks (United States Bureau of Labor Statistics, U.S. Department of Labor, 2018).

What might be a typical result of such an analysis? Surveying 100 clerical staff, a district may find out that department secretaries really spend most of their day as receptionists and information clerks whose job would include answering phones, greeting visitors, responding to inquiries from the public, and so forth.

USING TECHNOLOGY TO MANAGE HUMAN RESOURCES

Technology can play a significant role in increasing productivity at every level of the education system. Human resource management is no exception. From a human resource perspective, technology should assist with the following activities:

- Recruitment and screening of staff.
- Employee information: managing, maintaining, and reporting.
- Position control: tracking, managing, and authorizing district positions and related budget impacts.
- Job assignments: process for tracking, monitoring, and managing individual employee job assignments and related site/location; full-time equivalency; work calendars; and funding accounts.
- Compensation details: process for employee salary placement (linkage to salary schedules and special compensation such as stipends and/or longevity pay).
- Certificates/credentials: process to track teacher certification information.
- Process to document highly qualified teachers and ESSA compliance.
- Professional growth: tracking of educational course information by employee, including semester hours/units.
- Emergency contacts: process to update and maintain employee's emergency contact information (integration potential with current system, and if no current system, documentation of process to smooth transition).
- Health and welfare benefits: process for managing and tracking employee health benefits, including plan, policy, and associated premiums.
- Evaluations: process for tracking employee evaluation dates and outcomes.
- Substitute assignments: process for managing and tracking various substitute assignments, as well as linkages to rate of pay for each assignment.
- Service history: process of historical accounting of all previous job assignment history and associated service credit tracking.
- Reporting: access to timely, accurate, and comprehensive employee data.

In addition, there are a number of activities for which there may be shared responsibility with the school district's business office. Those activities include processes to:

- record and manage employee attendance and/or absence transactions by attendance period.
- manage employee leave balances such as sick leave, vacation, and personal necessity.

- account for substitute work and associated pay.
- authorize and post all employee leave associated with conference or other professional development, and related funding.
- authorize and post employee extra duty activity, pay, overtime, and stipend compensation.
- manage all compensation-related transactions by pay period.

Escalating costs, inadequate or missing authorizations, missing controls, and redundant processes are all reasons for implementing comprehensive human resource software. Human resource software should be dynamic, providing real-time data. It should be date-driven.

When an event such as a retirement or vacancy is known, it should be recorded in the system. Likewise, administrators should be able to ascertain vacancies, positions, absences, contractual obligations, and absences on any given day whether in the past or future. This is also crucial for reporting personnel positions and costs to boards of education and the public.

The process of obtaining an adequate *human resource software system* can be intimidating. Ideally, the software would be fully integrated with other software such as finance and business. As noted earlier, there are some key features that no software system should be without. Those include real-time process, date-driven data, and position control.

Furthermore, employees should have the ability to access the system for basic information. This saves staff time and provides a layer of transparency with regard to employee information. Textbox 8.2 is a checklist of the main features that should be considered when selecting a human resource software system.

TEXTBOX 8.2.   TECHNOLOGY DECISION-MAKING: ALIGNING HUMAN RESOURCES

Technology Decision-Making

What is the technology?

__Web browser-based
__Remote desktop—virtual desktop
__Silverlight
__HTML5
__How often are releases done?
__Are releases charged extra?
__History of releases

What does the district need?

__Financial/payroll
__Human resources/position control
__Budgeting driven from personnel costs
__Status change capabilities for tracking
__Accountability and authorization for all time sheet activities
__Student information system
__Data warehouse
__Integrated sub calling
__Integrated applicant tracking
__Everything integrated: one vendor fits all
__Best practices-only approach with ability to integrate where needed

What should pricing include (check all that apply)?

__New releases
__Training during implementation
__Training updates (webinars) after implementation
__Customer service support
__Implementation
__All data imports and exports
__Configurations (vendor will set limits)
__Flat annual fee for __ years
__Fixed range estimate on renewal fee for contract
__Pricing in one place, visible, no hidden fees: know exact price.

Services and support: Things to ask (check all that apply)

__Hours of operation and availability
__Trained professionals to meet the need
__User support request system
__Issue escalation process
__Dedicated primary contact person
__Enhancement request system
__Response time ranges
__User's forums
__Scheduled conferences or webinars
__Training for new releases
__Implementation schedule and milestones
__Assessment of district's understanding during implementation
__Role of the district in the process (e.g., implementation experts)

Source: Reprinted with permission from Digital Schools, LP, Volo, IL, and Salinas, CA (2012).

SHARED SERVICES

Another strategy that schools and school districts can utilize is *shared services*. This can have a direct or indirect impact on personnel needs. Consolidating services has resulted in cost savings and efficiencies in many states. Intergovernmental agreements for the delivery of low-incidence special education students and vocational education cooperatives are also common.

In some states, investment pools, cooperative bidding, state purchasing cooperatives, and shared fiscal services have also resulted in savings. Small school districts, in particular which have limited purchasing power, small staffs, and fewer funds to invest, are most likely to be the biggest beneficiaries of cooperative or shared services ventures. Following is a list of possible shared services in which school districts may engage that may impact human resource planning:

- Curriculum planning
- Custodial services
- Employee benefits
- Food services
- Staff recruitment
- Professional development
- Purchasing and procurement
- Special education
- Technology services
- Training and development
- Transportation services
- Vocational education

A more comprehensive approach to looking for efficiencies and increased productivity is the use of a performance audit. Performance audits can be used to determine how economical each of the school district's operations is and its efficiency. They can also be utilized to identify weaknesses in the system as well as compliance issues. Auditing firms or consultants familiar with the overall operations of school systems and their compliance issues most often execute performance audits.

SUMMARY

The use of technology in managing human resources will continue to grow. In the past, human resource management was driven by business side's need to account for personnel and budgets and to process payroll. In the future, the opposite will be true. The management of the human resources will drive the business side of education. The idea that human resources is basically a recruiting, employment, and evaluation function has a long past. Human resources departments of the future more closely resemble their private counterparts, providing an array of services and functions.

Human resources are the single biggest driver of costs in a school district. They are not only the most important educational resource but are also a school district's biggest asset. Performance, productivity, and efficiency are becoming important drivers of educational resources and human resources. Ensuring that school districts have the appropriate staff to be effective and at the same time efficient has prompted the use of process mapping and personnel/performance audits.

Outsourcing and shared services have also become an important component of resource management and personnel, where they are allowed by state law. With more and more emphasis on site-based management, all levels of administration now have input into staffing decisions and allocations.

CASE STUDY

Bottom Falls School District is growing rapidly. In 2012, the district was composed of one high school, one middle school, and three elementary schools. Today, the district has two high schools, two middle schools, and six elementary schools. The superintendent and board of education have decided it is now time to hire a full-time human resources director.

After careful consideration, they have asked you to assume the position. Your first step is to outline the duties and parameters of the department. The second step is to make recommendations regarding the implementation of a human resources software system.

Exercises and Discussion Questions

1. In the school system you work or reside, how are resource allocation decisions determined? Is there a process for evaluating whether resources result in increased student performance?
2. Utilizing the case study, how would you work with other administrators to ensure that staff is allocated and accounted for appropriately? What features would you look for in a software system for the human resources department?
3. In your professional life, what choices have you made with regard to allocating human resources to improve achievement? How did you determine whether they were successful?
4. What should be the role of the principal, superintendent, and board of education in allocating human resources and evaluating their effectiveness?

5. Using the process mapping technique outlined in the chapter, diagram your school district's hiring process. Review your diagram and reflect on the process. Are there any ways it could be improved, or are there any redundant steps that could be eliminated to make it more efficient?
6. If faced with the task of having to significantly reduce the expenditures in a school or school district, how would you go about it? How would human resources affect your decision?
7. What are the pros and cons of giving principals control over a school's human resource allocation?
8. Interview the administrator in charge of human resources in your district. Ascertain how well the current human resource software meets the needs of the district. What are the strengths and weaknesses of the software? Does the district utilize a position control system?

REFERENCES

Baroody, K. (2011). *Turning around the Nation's Lowest Performing Schools.* https://www.erstrategies.org/tap/turning_around_the_nations_lowest_performing_schools.

Brill, S. (2011). *Class Warfare: Inside the Fight to Fix America's Schools.* New York, NY: Simon & Schuster.

United States Bureau of Labor Statistics, U.S. Department of Labor. (2018). https://www.dol.gov/wb/stats/stats_data.htm.

Wilhite, R., Brierton, J., Schilling, C., and Tomal, D. (2017). *Leading with Resolve and Mastery.* Lanham, MD: Rowman & Littlefield Education.

Zirkel, P. (2011). State laws and guidelines for RTI: Additional implementation features. Communiqué Online. http://www.nasponline.org/publications/cq/39/7/professional-practice-state-laws.aspx

Epilogue

The evolution of the human resource function corresponds not only to the need to recruit quality staff but also to retain them. Additionally, the proliferation of laws and regulations affecting human resources has created a need for highly trained human resources professionals. The purpose of this epilogue is to summarize key points from the book and provide some of the major challenges that must be addressed if we are to be successful in the future.

There are many challenges facing school and corporate leaders, and our ability to manage employees is crucial for school and organizational success and outcomes. For example, even with the many initiatives schools are still failing to meet state and local standards. Across the nation schools continue to struggle to meet state and federal standards, and meeting these standards will become more challenging with less funding. Requests for additional funding and alternative testing programs will undoubtedly continue.

What is clear is that quality teaching is a primary focus. Both *No Child Left Behind* and *Race to the Top* focused on the training and employment of "highly qualified" staff. The implementation of *Every Student Succeeds Act* (ESSA) will raise this bar even higher by further focusing on how resources (people) at the school level impact student performance. Each state is now challenged to set its own educational goals and consequently how schools teach our children and young adults.

There continues to be a need for better collaboration among federal legislators. With the uncertainty of the Trump administration, educators continue to seek additional grants, resources, and expertise in building capacity and in pursuit of educational achievement. The struggle among educators and legislators regarding charter, private, and public schools, as well as new approaches to nontraditional schools and learning will continue. Undoubtedly educators need to be creative in managing their fiscal and human resources.

Not only are there resource issues, but administrators are faced with a myriad of *human resource and organizational challenges*. Administrators need to be equipped to recruit talented human resources to meet the educational demands of the school system. Therefore, the primary goal of human resource planning is to forecast the future needs of an organization and to ensure that all resources are obtained, anticipate changes in staffing, understand and stay current with federal and state laws and local district policies, and work with school community to match future needs and current organizational resources with future resources.

For example, financial constraints and ideology differences creating tensions between school boards and teacher unions continue to exist. There were many issues involved such as pay, benefits, class size, school closing procedures, and teacher evaluation. This has had a major impact on the community and students in our school districts. These conflicts impact sentiments toward unions, boards, and charter schools.

Given the progressing financial constraints, *compensation of employees* will continue to be an issue. Compensation represents about 80 percent or more of the school district's total budget. Educators and the board will need to carefully examine all the factors that motivate employees for good performance other than only relying upon compensation. They will also need to rely upon other creative compensation structures such as pay for performance, skills-based, knowledge-based, gain sharing, and merit plans that can be successfully utilized.

Proposing creative and different *compensation structures* will undoubtedly create increased conflict among the board, teachers, and unions as evidenced by schools across the nation. This will demand increased challenges in the collective bargaining process and call for all parties to work collaboratively to reach agreement. The collective bargaining process will need to be approached by all parties with good-faith intentions with the students' education as a foremost goal given the constraints of financial resources.

The *operations of the school* are highly dependent upon adequate safety and security, transportation, custodial care, facility maintenance, and meaningful auxiliary programs. All these programs impact the employees of a school district. Administrators and boards will need to continue to be resilient and creative in managing human resources to meet these needs and ensure all the proper certification is obtained.

While major metropolitan and large school districts have sophisticated human resource systems, smaller school systems are just recognizing the importance of such software. Technology will play an even bigger role in human resource planning in the future. Human resources will not only drive school business systems but also include features that will make it easier for administrators to predict and account for current and future staffing needs.

This is especially critical as more and more school districts relinquish more control to individual school sites. There is already a vast array of specialized screening instruments to filter out teacher candidates unlikely to be successful. This coming at the same time that fewer young adults are choosing to be teachers and administrators. Lastly, districts are finding creative solutions to addressing noncore functions in their schools such as outsourcing and sharing services.

In summary, future school leaders will need to learn how to do *more with less*. They will need to be skilled in process mapping and organizational improvement strategies to maximize resources, improve current operations, and manage human resources. This approach consists of identifying obstacles (wastes, bottlenecks, redundancies, delays, conflicts, inadequate technology and budget systems) that hinder efficiency among human resources and overall school management.

Educators will need to employ viable actions (value-added solutions) to address obstacles and provide accountability for fiscal stability and optimize human resource practices. The use of technology in the training, recruitment, screening, and management of staff as well as addressing legal requirements has become crucial for human resources departments to be successful. Finally, school leaders will need to assist all stakeholders in understanding the ever-important paradigm of efficient *fiscal stewardship* to maximize the limited resources for the education of students and meet the future demands of our community, government agencies, society, and workforce.

APPENDICES

Appendix A

Employee Rights[1]

Employees covered by the *National Labor Relations Act* (NLRA) are guaranteed the right to form, join, decertify, or assist a labor organization, and to bargain collectively through representatives of their own choosing, or to refrain from such activities. Employees may also join together to improve terms and conditions of employment without a union.

Employees covered by the NLRA are afforded certain rights to join together to improve their wages and working conditions, with or without a union.

UNION ACTIVITY

Employees have the right to attempt to form a union where none currently exists, or to decertify a union that has lost the support of employees.

Examples of employee rights include:

- Forming, or attempting to form, a union in your workplace;
- Joining a union whether the union is recognized by your employer or not;
- Assisting a union in organizing your fellow employees;
- Refusing to do any or all of these things.
- To be fairly represented by a union.

ACTIVITY OUTSIDE A UNION

Employees who are not represented by a union also have rights under the NLRA. Specifically, the *National Labor Relations Board* protects the rights of employees to engage in "protected concerted activity," which is when two

Appendix A

or more employees take action for their mutual aid or protection regarding terms and conditions of employment. A single employee may also engage in protected concerted activity if he or she is acting on the authority of other employees, bringing group complaints to the employer's attention, trying to induce group action, or seeking to prepare for group action.

A few examples of protected concerted activities are:

- Two or more employees addressing their employer about improving their pay.
- Two or more employees discussing work-related issues beyond pay, such as safety concerns, with each other.
- An employee speaking to an employer on behalf of one or more coworkers about improving workplace conditions.

WHO IS COVERED?

Most employees in the private sector are covered by the NLRA. However, the act specifically excludes individuals who are:

- employed by federal, state, or local government
- employed as agricultural laborers
- employed in the domestic service of any person or family in a home
- employed by a parent or spouse
- employed as an independent contractor
- employed as a supervisor (supervisors who have been discriminated against for refusing to violate the NLRA may be covered)
- employed by an employer subject to the Railway Labor Act, such as rail-roads and airlines
- employed by any other person who is not an employer as defined in the NLRA

NOTE

1. Source: https://www.nlrb.gov/rights-we-protect/employee-rights.

Appendix B

Employer and Union Rights and Obligations[1]

The law forbids employers from interfering with employees in the exercise of rights to form, join, or assist a labor organization for collective bargaining or from working together to improve terms and conditions of employment or refraining from any such activity. Similarly, labor organizations may not interfere with employees in the exercise of these rights.

The *National Labor Relations Act* (NLRA) forbids employers from interfering with, restraining, or coercing employees in the exercise of rights relating to organizing, forming, joining, or assisting a labor organization for collective bargaining purposes, or from working together to improve terms and conditions of employment, or refraining from any such activity. Similarly, labor organizations may not restrain or coerce employees in the exercise of these rights.

Examples of employer conduct that violates the law:

- Threatening employees with loss of jobs or benefits if they join or vote for a union or engage in protected concerted activity.
- Threatening to close the plant if employees select a union to represent them.
- Questioning employees about their union sympathies or activities in circumstances that tend to interfere with, restrain, or coerce employees in the exercise of their rights under the NLRA.
- Promising benefits to employees to discourage their union support.
- Transferring, laying off, terminating, and assigning employees more difficult work tasks, or otherwise punishing employees because they engaged in union or protected concerted activity.
- Transferring, laying off, terminating, and assigning employees more difficult work tasks, or otherwise punishing employees because they filed

unfair labor practice charges or participated in an investigation conducted by *National Labor Relations Board* (NLRB).

Examples of labor organization conduct that violates the law:

- Threats to employees that they will lose their jobs unless they support the union.
- Seeking the suspension, discharge, or other punishment of an employee for not being a union member even if the employee has paid or offered to pay a lawful initiation fee and periodic fees thereafter.
- Refusing to process a grievance because an employee has criticized union officials or because an employee is not a member of the union in states where union security clauses are not permitted.
- Fining employees who have validly resigned from the union for engaging in protected concerted activities following their resignation or for crossing an unlawful picket line.
- Engaging in picket line misconduct, such as threatening, assaulting, or barring nonstrikers from the employer's premises.
- Striking over issues unrelated to employment terms and conditions or coercively enmeshing neutrals into a labor dispute.

WHAT RULES GOVERN COLLECTIVE BARGAINING FOR A CONTRACT?

After employees choose a union as a bargaining representative, the employer and union are required to meet at reasonable times to bargain in good faith about wages, hours, vacation time, insurance, safety practices, and other mandatory subjects. Some managerial decisions such as subcontracting, relocation, and other operational changes may not be mandatory subjects of bargaining, but the employer must bargain about the decision's effects on unit employees.

It is an *unfair labor practice* for either party to refuse to bargain collectively with the other, but parties are not compelled to reach agreement or make concessions.

If after sufficient good faith efforts, no agreement can be reached, the employer may declare impasse, and then implement the last offer presented to the union. However, the union may disagree that true impasse has been reached and file a charge of an unfair labor practice for failure to bargain in good faith. The NLRB will determine whether true impasse was reached based on the history of negotiations and the understandings of both parties.

If the Agency finds that impasse was not reached, the employer will be asked to return to the bargaining table. In an extreme case, the NLRB may seek a federal court order to force the employer to bargain.

The parties' obligations do not end when the contract expires. They must bargain in good faith for a successor contract, or for the termination of the agreement, while terms of the expired contract continue.

A party wishing to end the contract must notify the other party in writing sixty days before the expiration date or sixty days before the proposed termination. The party must offer to meet and confer with the other party and notify the Federal Mediation and Conciliation Service of the existence of a dispute if no agreement has been reached by that time.

HOW IS "GOOD-FAITH" BARGAINING DETERMINED?

There are hundreds, perhaps thousands, of NLRB cases dealing with the issue of the duty to bargain in good faith. In determining whether a party is bargaining in good faith, the board will look at the totality of the circumstances. The duty to bargain in good faith is an obligation to participate actively in the deliberations so as to indicate a present intention to find a basis for agreement. This implies both an open mind and a sincere desire to reach an agreement, as well as a sincere effort to reach a common ground.

The additional requirement to bargain in "good faith" was incorporated to ensure that a party did not come to the bargaining table and simply go through the motions. There are objective criteria that the NLRB will review to determine if the parties are honoring their obligation to bargain in good faith, such as whether the party is willing to meet at reasonable times and intervals and whether the party is represented by someone who has the authority to make decisions at the table.

Conduct away from the bargaining table may also be relevant. For instance, if an employer were to make a unilateral change in the terms and conditions of employees' employment without bargaining, that would be an indication of bad faith.

NOTE

1. Source: https://www.nlrb.gov/rights-we-protect/employerunion-rights-obligations.

Appendix C

Summary of the Major Laws of the *Department of Labor*[1]

The *Department of Labor* (DOL) administers and enforces more than 180 federal laws. These mandates and the regulations that implement them cover many workplace activities for about 10 million employers and 125 million workers.

Following is a brief description of many of DOL's principal statutes most commonly applicable to businesses, job seekers, workers, retirees, contractors, and grantees. This brief summary is intended to acquaint you with the major labor laws and not to offer a detailed exposition. For authoritative information and references to fuller descriptions on these laws, you should consult the statutes and regulations themselves.

Employment Laws Assistance provides a list of selected U.S. Department of Labor laws and regulations with links to related compliance assistance activities. The DOL compliance assistance website offers complete information on how to comply with federal employment laws.

Rulemaking and Regulations provide brief descriptions of and links to various sources of information on DOL's rulemaking activities and regulations.

WAGES AND HOURS

The *Fair Labor Standards Act* (FLSA) prescribes standards for wages and overtime pay, which affect most private and public employment. The act is administered by the Wage and Hour Division. It requires employers to pay covered employees, who are not otherwise exempt, at least the federal minimum wage and overtime pay of one-and-one-half times the regular rate of pay. For nonagricultural operations, it restricts the hours that children under age sixteen can work and forbids the employment of children under age eighteen in certain jobs deemed too dangerous. It prohibits the employment of children under age sixteen in agricultural operations during school hours and in certain jobs deemed too dangerous.

The Wage and Hour Division also enforces the labor standards provisions of the Immigration and Nationality Act (INA) that apply to aliens authorized to work in the United States under certain nonimmigrant visa programs (H-1B, H-1B1, H-1C, H2A).

WORKPLACE SAFETY AND HEALTH

The *Occupational Safety and Health (OSH) Act* is administered by the Occupational Safety and Health Administration (OSHA). Safety and health conditions in most private industries are regulated by OSHA or OSHA-approved state programs, which also cover public sector employers. Employers covered by the OSH Act must comply with the regulations and the safety and health standards promulgated by OSHA. Employers also have a general duty under the OSH Act to provide their employees with work and a workplace free from recognized, serious hazards. OSHA enforces the OSH Act through workplace inspections and investigations. Compliance assistance and other cooperative programs are also available.

WORKERS' COMPENSATION

The *Longshore and Harbor Workers' Compensation Act* (LHWCA), administered by The Office of Workers Compensation Programs (OWCP), provides for compensation and medical care to certain maritime employees (including a longshore worker or other person in longshore operations and any harbor worker, including a ship repairer, shipbuilder, and shipbreaker) and to qualified dependent survivors of such employees who are disabled or die due to injuries that occur on the navigable waters of the United States or in adjoining areas customarily used in loading, unloading, repairing, or building a vessel.

The *Energy Employees Occupational Illness Compensation Program Act* (EEOICPA) is a compensation program that provides a lump-sum payment of $150,000 and prospective medical benefits to employees (or certain of their survivors) of the Department of Energy and its contractors and subcontractors as a result of cancer caused by exposure to radiation, or certain illnesses caused by exposure to beryllium or silica incurred in the performance of duty, as well as a payment of a lump sum of $50,000 and prospective medical benefits to individuals (or certain of their survivors) determined by the Department of Justice to be eligible for compensation as uranium workers under section 5 of the Radiation Exposure Compensation Act.

The *Federal Employees' Compensation Act* (FECA), 5 U.S.C. 8101 et seq., establishes a comprehensive and exclusive workers' compensation program, which pays compensation for the disability or death of a federal employee resulting from personal injury sustained while in the performance of duty. The FECA, administered by OWCP, provides benefits for wage loss compensation for total or partial disability, schedule awards for permanent loss or loss of use of specified members of the body, related medical costs, and vocational rehabilitation.

The *Black Lung Benefits Act* (BLBA) provides monthly cash payments and medical benefits to coal miners totally disabled from pneumoconiosis ("black lung disease") arising from their employment in the nation's coal mines. The statute also provides monthly benefits to a deceased miner's survivors if the miner's death was due to black lung disease.

EMPLOYEE BENEFIT SECURITY

The *Employee Retirement Income Security Act* (ERISA) regulates employers who offer pension or welfare benefit plans for their employees. Title I of ERISA is administered by the Employee Benefits Security Administration (EBSA) (formerly the Pension and Welfare Benefits Administration) and imposes a wide range of fiduciary, disclosure, and reporting requirements on fiduciaries of pension and welfare benefit plans and on others having dealings with these plans. These provisions preempt many similar state laws.

Under Title IV, certain employers and plan administrators must fund an insurance system to protect certain kinds of retirement benefits, with premiums paid to the federal government's *Pension Benefit Guaranty Corporation* (PBGC). EBSA also administers reporting requirements for continuation of health care provisions, required under the Comprehensive Omnibus Budget Reconciliation Act of 1985 and the health care portability requirements on group plans under the Health Insurance Portability and Accountability Act.

UNIONS AND THEIR MEMBERS

The *Labor-Management Reporting and Disclosure Act* (LMRDA) of 1959 (also known as the Landrum-Griffin Act) deals with the relationship between a union and its members. It protects union funds and promotes union democracy by requiring labor organizations to file annual financial reports; by requiring union officials, employers, and labor consultants to file reports regarding certain labor relations practices; and by establishing standards for the election of union officers. The act is administered by the *Office of Labor-Management Standards*.

EMPLOYEE PROTECTION

Most labor and public safety laws and many environmental laws mandate whistle-blower protections for employees who complain about violations of the law by their employers. Remedies can include job reinstatement and payment of back wages. *OSHA* enforces the whistle-blower protections in most laws.

UNIFORMED SERVICES EMPLOYMENT AND REEMPLOYMENT RIGHTS ACT

Certain persons who serve in the armed forces have a right to reemployment with the employer they were with when they entered service. This includes those called up from the reserves or National Guard. These rights are administered by the *Veterans' Employment and Training Service* (VETS).

EMPLOYEE POLYGRAPH PROTECTION ACT

This law bars most employers from using lie detectors on employees but permits polygraph tests only in limited circumstances. It is administered by the Wage and Hour Division.

GARNISHMENT OF WAGES

Garnishment of employee wages by employers is regulated under the Consumer Credit Protection Act, which is administered by the Wage and Hour Division.

THE FAMILY AND MEDICAL LEAVE ACT

Administered by the Wage and Hour Division, the *Family and Medical Leave Act* requires employers of fifty or more employees to give up to twelve weeks of unpaid, job-protected leave to eligible employees for the birth or adoption of a child or for the serious illness of the employee or a spouse, child, or parent.

VETERANS' PREFERENCE

Veterans and other eligible persons have special employment rights with the federal government. They are provided preference in initial hiring and protection in reductions in force. Claims of violation of these rights are investigated by the VETS.

GOVERNMENT CONTRACTS, GRANTS, OR FINANCIAL AID

Recipients of government contracts, grants, or financial aid are subject to wage, hour, benefits, and safety and health standards under:

- The Davis-Bacon Act, which requires payment of prevailing wages and benefits to employees of contractors engaged in federal government construction projects;
- The McNamara-O'Hara Service Contract Act, which sets wage rates and other labor standards for employees of contractors furnishing services to the federal government;
- The Walsh-Healey Public Contracts Act, which requires payment of minimum wages and other labor standards by contractors providing materials and supplies to the federal government;
- Administration and enforcement of these laws are by the Wage and Hour Division. The *Office of Federal Contract Compliance Programs* administers and enforces three federal contract-based civil rights laws that require most federal contractors and subcontractors, as well as federally assisted construction contractors, to provide equal employment opportunity. The *Office of the Assistant Secretary for Administration and Management's* Civil Rights Center administers and enforces several federal assistance-based civil rights laws requiring recipients of federal financial assistance from Department of Labor to provide equal opportunity.

MIGRANT AND SEASONAL AGRICULTURAL WORKERS

The *Migrant and Seasonal Agricultural Worker Protection Act* (MSPA) regulates the hiring and employment activities of agricultural employers, farm labor contractors, and associations using migrant and seasonal agricultural workers. The MSPA prescribes wage protections, housing and transportation safety standards, farm labor contractor registration requirements, and disclosure requirements. The Wage and Hour Division administers this law.

The FLSA exempts agricultural workers from overtime premium pay but requires the payment of the minimum wage to workers employed on larger farms (farms employing more than approximately seven full-time workers).

The FLSA has special child-labor regulations that apply to agricultural employment; children under sixteen are forbidden to work during school hours and in certain jobs deemed too dangerous. Children employed on their families' farms are exempt from these regulations. The Wage and Hour Division administers this law. OSHA also has special safety and health standards that may apply to agricultural operations.

The INA requires employers who want to use foreign temporary workers on H-2A visas to get a labor certificate from the Employment and Training Administration certifying that there are not sufficient, able, willing, and qualified U.S. workers available to do the work. The labor standards protections of the H-2A program are enforced by the Wage and Hour Division.

MINE SAFETY AND HEALTH

The Federal Mine Safety and Health Act of 1977 (Mine Act) covers all people who work on mine property. The Mine Safety and Health Administration (MSHA) administers this Act.

The *Mine Act* holds mine operators responsible for the safety and health of miners, provides for the setting of mandatory safety and health standards, mandates miners' training requirements, prescribes penalties for violations, and enables inspectors to close dangerous mines. The safety and health standards address numerous hazards including roof falls, flammable and explosive gases, fire, electricity, equipment rollovers and maintenance, airborne contaminants, noise, and respirable dust. MSHA enforces safety and health requirements at more than 13,000 mines, investigates mine accidents, and offers mine operators training and technical and compliance assistance.

CONSTRUCTION

Several agencies administer programs related solely to the construction industry. OSHA has special occupational safety and health standards for construction; the Wage and Hour Division, under Davis-Bacon and related acts, requires payment of prevailing wages and benefits; the *Office of Federal Contract Compliance Programs* enforces Executive Order 11246, which requires federal construction contractors and subcontractors, as well as federally assisted construction contractors, to provide equal employment opportunity; the anti-kickback section of the Copeland Act precludes a federal contractor from inducing any employee to sacrifice any part of the compensation required.

TRANSPORTATION

Most laws with labor provisions regulating the transportation industry are administered by agencies outside the *Department of Labor*. However, long-shoring and maritime industry safety and health standards are issued and enforced by OSHA. The LHWCA requires employers to assure that workers' compensation is funded and available to eligible employees. In addition, the rights of employees in the mass transit industry are protected when federal funds are used to acquire, improve, or operate a transit system. Under the Federal Transit Law, the *Department of Labor* is responsible for approving employee protection arrangements before the *Department of Transportation* can release funds to grantees.

PLANT CLOSINGS AND LAYOFFS

Such occurrences may be subject to the *Worker Adjustment and Retraining Notification (WARN) Act*. WARN offers employees early warning of impending layoffs or plant closings. The *Employment and Training Administration* (ETA) provides information to the public on WARN, though neither ETA nor the Department of Labor has administrative responsibility for the statute, which is enforced through private action in the federal courts.

ADVISORIES

For more details and guidance on laws and regulations covered in this fact sheet, call the appropriate Department of Labor agency listed in your phone book under U.S. Government.

Other federal agencies besides the Department of Labor enforce laws and regulations that affect employers.

Statutes that ensure nondiscrimination in employment are generally enforced by the Equal Employment Opportunity Commission.

The Taft-Hartley Act regulates a wide range of employer–employee conduct and is administered by the National Labor Relations Board.

For more information on these laws, consult these agencies; they are listed in your phone book under U.S. Government.

NOTE

1. Source: United States Bureau of Labor Statistics. http://www.dol.gov/opa/aboutdol/law.

Appendix D

Laws Enforced by the Equal Employment Opportunity Commission[1]

TITLE VII OF THE CIVIL RIGHTS ACT OF 1964 (TITLE VII)

This law makes it illegal to discriminate against someone on the basis of race, color, religion, national origin, or sex. The law also makes it illegal to retaliate against a person because the person complained about discrimination, filed a charge of discrimination, or participated in an employment discrimination investigation or lawsuit. The law also requires that employers reasonably accommodate applicants' and employees' sincerely held religious practices, unless doing so would impose an undue hardship on the operation of the employer's business.

- The Pregnancy Discrimination Act

    This law amended Title VII to make it illegal to discriminate against a woman because of pregnancy, childbirth, or a medical condition related to pregnancy or childbirth. The law also makes it illegal to retaliate against a person because the person complained about discrimination, filed a charge of discrimination, or participated in an employment discrimination investigation or lawsuit.

- The Equal Pay Act of 1963

    This law makes it illegal to pay different wages to men and women if they perform equal work in the same workplace. The law also makes it illegal to retaliate against a person because the person complained about discrimination, filed a charge of discrimination, or participated in an employment discrimination investigation or lawsuit.

* The Age Discrimination in Employment Act of 1967

   This law protects people who are forty or older from discrimination because of age. The law also makes it illegal to retaliate against a person because the person complained about discrimination, filed a charge of discrimination, or participated in an employment discrimination investigation or lawsuit.

* Title I of the Americans with Disabilities Act of 1990

   This law makes it illegal to discriminate against a qualified person with a disability in the private sector and in state and local governments. The law also makes it illegal to retaliate against a person because the person complained about discrimination, filed a charge of discrimination, or participated in an employment discrimination investigation or lawsuit. The law also requires that employers reasonably accommodate the known physical or mental limitations of an otherwise qualified individual with a disability who is an applicant or employee, unless doing so would impose an undue hardship on the operation of the employer's business.

* Sections 102 and 103 of the Civil Rights Act of 1991

   Among other things, this law amends Title VII and the ADA to permit jury trials and compensatory and punitive damage awards in intentional discrimination cases.

* Sections 501 and 505 of the Rehabilitation Act of 1973

   This law makes it illegal to discriminate against a qualified person with a disability in the federal government. The law also makes it illegal to retaliate against a person because the person complained about discrimination, filed a charge of discrimination, or participated in an employment discrimination investigation or lawsuit. The law also requires that employers reasonably accommodate the known physical or mental limitations of an otherwise qualified individual with a disability who is an applicant or employee, unless doing so would impose an undue hardship on the operation of the employer's business.

- The Genetic Information Nondiscrimination Act of 2008

  Effective—November 21, 2009.
  This law makes it illegal to discriminate against employees or applicants because of genetic information. Genetic information includes information about an individual's genetic tests and the genetic tests of an individual's family members, as well as information about any disease, disorder, or condition of an individual's family members (i.e., an individual's family medical history). The law also makes it illegal to retaliate against a person because the person complained about discrimination, filed a charge of discrimination, or participated in an employment discrimination investigation or lawsuit.

NOTE

1. Source: Equal Employment Opportunity Commission. http://www.eeoc.gov/laws/statutes/index.cfm.

Appendix E

Prohibited Employment Policies and Practices[1]

Under the laws enforced by Equal Employment Opportunity Commission (EEOC), it is illegal to discriminate against someone (applicant or employee) because of that person's race, color, religion, sex (including pregnancy), national origin, age (forty or older), disability, or genetic information. It is also illegal to retaliate against a person because he or she complained about discrimination, filed a charge of discrimination, or participated in an employment discrimination investigation or lawsuit.

The law forbids discrimination in every aspect of employment.

The laws enforced by EEOC prohibit an employer or other covered entity from using neutral employment policies and practices that have a disproportionately negative effect on applicants or employees of a particular race, color, religion, sex (including pregnancy), or national origin, or on an individual with a disability or class of individuals with disabilities, if the policies or practices at issue are not job-related and necessary to the operation of the business. The laws enforced by EEOC also prohibit an employer from using neutral employment policies and practices that have a disproportionately negative impact on applicants or employees age forty or older, if the policies or practices at issue are not based on a reasonable factor other than age.

JOB ADVERTISEMENTS

It is illegal for an employer to publish a job advertisement that shows a preference for or discourages someone from applying for a job because of his or her race, color, religion, sex (including pregnancy), national origin, age (forty or older), disability, or genetic information.

For example, a help-wanted ad that seeks "females" or "recent college graduates" may discourage men and people over forty from applying and may violate the law.

RECRUITMENT

It is also illegal for an employer to recruit new employees in a way that discriminates against them because of their race, color, religion, sex (including pregnancy), national origin, age (forty or older), disability, or genetic information.

For example, an employer's reliance on word-of-mouth recruitment by its mostly Hispanic workforce may violate the law if the result is that almost all new hires are Hispanic.

APPLICATION AND HIRING

It is illegal for an employer to discriminate against a job applicant because of his or her race, color, religion, sex (including pregnancy), national origin, age (forty or older), disability, or genetic information. For example, an employer may not refuse to give employment applications to people of a certain race.

An employer may not base hiring decisions on stereotypes and assumptions about a person's race, color, religion, sex (including pregnancy), national origin, age (forty or older), disability or genetic information.

If an employer requires job applicants to take a test, the test must be necessary and related to the job, and the employer may not exclude people of a particular race, color, religion, sex (including pregnancy), national origin, or individuals with disabilities. In addition, the employer may not use a test that excludes applicants age forty or older if the test is not based on a reasonable factor other than age.

If a job applicant with a disability needs an accommodation (such as a sign language interpreter) to apply for a job, the employer is required to provide the accommodation, so long as the accommodation does not cause the employer significant difficulty or expense.

JOB REFERRALS

It is illegal for an employer, employment agency, or union to take into account a person's race, color, religion, sex (including pregnancy), national origin, age (forty or older), disability, or genetic information when making decisions about job referrals.

JOB ASSIGNMENTS AND PROMOTIONS

It is illegal for an employer to make decisions about job assignments and promotions based on an employee's race, color, religion, sex (including pregnancy), national origin, age (forty or older), disability, or genetic information. For example, an employer may not give preference to employees of a certain race when making shift assignments and may not segregate employees of a particular national origin from other employees or from customers.

An employer may not base assignment and promotion decisions on stereotypes and assumptions about a person's race, color, religion, sex (including pregnancy), national origin, age (forty or older), disability, or genetic information.

If an employer requires employees to take a test before making decisions about assignments or promotions, the test may not exclude people of a particular race, color, religion, sex (including pregnancy), or national origin, or individuals with disabilities, unless the employer can show that the test is necessary and related to the job. In addition, the employer may not use a test that excludes employees age forty or older if the test is not based on a reasonable factor other than age.

PAY AND BENEFITS

It is illegal for an employer to discriminate against an employee in the payment of wages or employee benefits on the basis of race, color, religion, sex (including pregnancy), national origin, age (forty or older), disability, or genetic information. Employee benefits include sick and vacation leave, insurance, access to overtime as well as overtime pay, and retirement programs. For example, an employer may not pay Hispanic workers less than African American workers because of their national origin, and men and women in the same workplace must be given equal pay for equal work.

In some situations, an employer may be allowed to reduce some employee benefits for older workers but only if the cost of providing the reduced benefits is the same as the cost of providing benefits to younger workers.

DISCIPLINE AND DISCHARGE

An employer may not take into account a person's race, color, religion, sex (including pregnancy), national origin, age (forty or older), disability, or genetic information when making decisions about discipline or discharge. For example, if two employees commit a similar offense, an employer may not discipline them differently because of their race, color, religion, sex (including pregnancy), national origin, age (forty or older), disability, or genetic information.

When deciding which employees will be laid off, an employer may not choose the oldest workers because of their age.

Employers also may not discriminate when deciding which workers to recall after a layoff.

EMPLOYMENT REFERENCES

It is illegal for an employer to give a negative or false employment reference (or refuse to give a reference) because of a person's race, color, religion, sex (including pregnancy), national origin, age (forty or older), disability, or genetic information.

REASONABLE ACCOMMODATION AND DISABILITY

The law requires that an employer provide reasonable accommodation to an employee or job applicant with a disability, unless doing so would cause significant difficulty or expense for the employer.

A reasonable accommodation is any change in the workplace (or in the ways things are usually done) to help a person with a disability apply for a job, perform the duties of a job, or enjoy the benefits and privileges of employment.

Reasonable accommodation might include, for example, providing a ramp for a wheelchair user or providing a reader or interpreter for a blind or deaf employee or applicant.

REASONABLE ACCOMMODATION AND RELIGION

The law requires an employer to reasonably accommodate an employee's religious beliefs or practices, unless doing so would cause difficulty or expense for the employer. This means an employer may have to make reasonable adjustments at work that will allow the employee to practice his or her religion, such as allowing an employee to voluntarily swap shifts with a coworker so that he or she can attend religious services.

TRAINING AND APPRENTICESHIP PROGRAMS

It is illegal for a training or apprenticeship program to discriminate on the basis of race, color, religion, sex (including pregnancy), national origin, age (forty or older), disability, or genetic information. For example, an employer may not deny training opportunities to African American employees because of their race.

In some situations, an employer may be allowed to set age limits for participation in an apprenticeship program.

HARASSMENT

It is illegal to harass an employee because of race, color, religion, sex (including pregnancy), national origin, age (forty or older), disability, or genetic information.

It is also illegal to harass someone because they have complained about discrimination, filed a charge of discrimination, or participated in an employment discrimination investigation or lawsuit.

Harassment can take the form of slurs, graffiti, offensive or derogatory comments, or other verbal or physical conduct. Sexual harassment (including unwelcome sexual advances, requests for sexual favors, and other conduct of a sexual nature) is also unlawful. Although the law does not prohibit simple teasing, offhand comments, or isolated incidents that are not very serious, harassment is illegal if it is so frequent or severe that it creates a hostile or offensive work environment or if it results in an adverse employment decision (such as the victim being fired or demoted).

The harasser can be the victim's supervisor, a supervisor in another area, a coworker, or someone who is not an employee of the employer, such as a client or customer. Harassment outside of the workplace may also be illegal if there is a link with the workplace. For example, if a supervisor harasses an employee while driving the employee to a meeting.

TERMS AND CONDITIONS OF EMPLOYMENT

The law makes it illegal for an employer to make any employment decision because of a person's race, color, religion, sex (including pregnancy), national origin, age (forty or older), disability, or genetic information. That means an employer may not discriminate when it comes to such things as hiring, firing, promotions, and pay. It also means an employer may not discriminate, for example, when granting breaks, approving leave, assigning work stations, or setting any other term or condition of employment—however small.

PREEMPLOYMENT INQUIRIES (GENERAL)

As a general rule, the information obtained and requested through the preemployment process should be limited to those essential for determining if a person is qualified for the job; whereas, information regarding race, sex, national origin, age, and religion are irrelevant in such determinations.

Employers are explicitly prohibited from making preemployment inquiries about disability.

Although state and federal equal opportunity laws do not clearly forbid employers from making preemployment inquiries that relate to, or disproportionately screen out members based on, race, color, sex, national origin, religion, or age, such inquiries may be used as evidence of an employer's intent to discriminate unless the questions asked can be justified by some business purpose.

Therefore, inquiries about organizations, clubs, societies, and lodges of which an applicant may be a member or any other questions, which may indicate the applicant's race, sex, national origin, disability status, age, religion, color, or ancestry, if answered, should generally be avoided.

Similarly, employers should not ask for a photograph of an applicant. If needed for identification purposes, a photograph may be obtained after an offer of employment is made and accepted.

Preemployment inquiries are regarding:

- Race
- Height and Weight
- Credit rating or economic status
- Religious affiliation or beliefs
- Citizenship
- Marital status, number of children
- Gender
- Arrest and conviction
- Security/background checks for certain religious or ethnic groups
- Disability
- Medical questions and examinations

DRESS CODE

In general, an employer may establish a dress code that applies to all employees or employees within certain job categories. However, there are a few possible exceptions.

While an employer may require all workers to follow a uniform dress code even if the dress code conflicts with some workers' ethnic beliefs or practices, a dress code must not treat some employees less favorably because of their national origin. For example, a dress code that prohibits certain kinds of ethnic dress, such as traditional African or East Indian attire, but otherwise permits casual dress would treat some employees less favorably because of their national origin.

Moreover, if the dress code conflicts with an employee's religious practices and the employee requests an accommodation, the employer must modify the dress code or permit an exception to the dress code unless doing so would result in undue hardship.

Similarly, if an employee requests an accommodation to the dress code because of his or her disability, the employer must modify the dress code or permit an exception to the dress code, unless doing so would result in undue hardship.

CONSTRUCTIVE DISCHARGE AND FORCED TO RESIGN

Discriminatory practices under the laws EEOC enforces also include constructive discharge or forcing an employee to resign by making the work environment so intolerable that a reasonable person would not be able to stay.

NOTE

1. Source: Equal Employment Opportunity Commission. http://www.eeoc.gov/laws/practices/index.cfm.

Index

About the Authors

Daniel R. Tomal, PhD, is a distinguished professor of Leadership at Concordia University Chicago and has published over twenty books (several with Rowman & Littlefield) and over 200 articles and studies. He has testified before the United States Congress and has consulted for numerous schools and organizations and quoted in many journals such as the *Wall Street Journal*, *Human Resource Development Quarterly*, and the *Chicago Tribune*. He is a former school administrator, high school teacher, and corporate vice president where he was in charge of human resources. He has made guest appearances on many national and local television and radio shows such as *CBS This Morning*, *NBC Cover to Cover*, *ABC News*, *Les Brown*, *Joan Rivers*, *Tom Snyder*, *Success Solutions International*, *Chicago Talks*, and so on.

Craig A. Schilling, EdD, is currently a professor of Educational Leadership at Concordia University Chicago, River Forest, Illinois. He has been a public school administrator, systems analyst, and CEO. He has consulted for numerous school districts and has spoken and presented at over 100 workshops and training seminars throughout the United States, Australia, Canada, and the Caribbean. Craig has received numerous national awards for his contributions to school finance and research. He has published five books (many of them with Rowman & Littlefield). He is the recipient of multiple national awards for his service to education and research.